Pe

re Clair, Elizabeth Raymond Barker, Frederick Raymond Barker

Father Milleriot

The Ravignan of the working men of Paris

Pe

re Clair, Elizabeth Raymond Barker, Frederick Raymond Barker

Father Milleriot
The Ravignan of the working men of Paris

ISBN/EAN: 9783742835857

Manufactured in Europe, USA, Canada, Australia, Japa

Cover: Foto ©Lupo / pixelio.de

Manufactured and distributed by brebook publishing software (www.brebook.com)

Pe

re Clair, Elizabeth Raymond Barker, Frederick Raymond Barker

Father Milleriot

FATHER MILLERIOT,

THE

Ravignan of the Working Men of Paris.

FROM THE FRENCH OF THE

REV. PÈRE CLAIR, S.J.,

WITH THE SPECIAL PERMISSION OF THE AUTHOR,

BY

MRS. F. RAYMOND-BARKER.

LONDON:
THOMAS RICHARDSON AND SON,
AND DERBY.
1882.

AUTHOR'S PREFACE.

ON the 30th of June, 1880, during the execution of the unjust decrees of March, and the violent expulsion of the Jesuit Fathers from their residence in the rue de Sèvres, one of their number, a priest, eighty years of age, but still upright and vigorous, quitted his cell about seven in the morning, passed through the throng of police agents which filled the court, and as they blocked the outer gate, said to the wondering *sergents de ville* and the agitated crowd, "Make way; I am half an hour late at St. Sulpice."

It was FATHER LOUIS MILLERIOT, who on this day, as on every other, repaired to his confessional in the Church of St. Sulpice, where for forty years he had instructed the ignorant and converted sinners.

For the disciple showed himself worthy of his Master, and could meet his enemies with the same testimony to his beneficent mission,

Pauperes evangelizabantur. But he too was proscribed, notwithstanding; and whilst he and his companions in the apostolate were cast into the street as malefactors, the Living God in the Holy Eucharist was made prisoner as in the garden, and sealed and guarded as in the tomb.

On the morrow, from his confessional near the principal entrance of the church, Father Milleriot heard the sound of a vast multitude thronging into the holy place. Thousands of men,—some among them men of the highest rank,—were come to make an act of reparation to Jesus in the Most Holy Sacrament. The Sacred Host was to have been carried by Mgr. Richard, Archbishop of Larissa, and Coadjutor of the Cardinal Archbishop of Paris, from the Church of the Jesuit Fathers, to that of St. Sulpice; the Prefect of Police, however, displeased at seeing the immense crowds assembled to do honour to the Blessed Sacrament by a religious manifestation, prohibited Its removal from the rue de Sèvres. It was therefore transferred from the church, into a inner chapel of the Residence, by Mgr. Richard. Then, proceeding to St. Sulpice, the Archbishop gave solemn Benediction to the multitudes which filled the church and the great square in front of it. And thus, as always in the history of the Catholic Church, "*Crucifigatur*" was followed by "*Alleluia.*"

Six months later, a multitude, equal in numbers, followed the same road. This time it escorted the funeral hearse used only for the poor, and upon which lay a coffin whose only decoration was the stole of a priest. After the triumph of the insulted God, followed that of His venerable servant, who, in death, received solemn homage in the same place where he had, in life, been unwearied in doing good, and where also he had suffered wrongfully.

It is not he, assuredly, who claims our pity, but those who, whether from hate or cowardice, afflicted the last days of his devoted life, and hastened its end. He forgave them all. May God forgive them also. Their folly being greater than their sin, they claim more pity than indignation.

And if, like the Jews of old, they knew not what they did, and acted blindly, some few among them are beginning to open their eyes, to accuse themselves in private, excuse themselves in public, and throw the blame of their deeds upon each other. We would beg those who wish to learn the rights of the case, to read these pages, in which they will learn to know, *as they are*, those whom they have calumniated, and to respect those whom they have outraged in their rights, their reputation, and their liberty.

At the same time, it is more especially to the many friends of Father Milleriot that we humbly offer this book, happy if it may aid in tempering their regret, by placing before them an approximately faithful portrait of this eminently good man.

Before his departure, he expressed a wish, entirely free from any personal feeling, that the record and the experiences of his long life should not all be lost. May the following pages, in which a portion of this record is enshrined, further the realization of his ardent desire to promote, even after death, the good of souls and the glory of God.

Ch. Clair, S.J.

NOTICE BY THE TRANSLATOR.

The following account is occasionally shortened from the original, while, on the other hand, one or two trifling additions from other reliable sources have been made. The closing incident of Chapter VIII., for instance, is taken from the "Notice" of Father Clair's work in the *Bulletin Bibliographique* of the *Revue du Monde Catholique* for July 15, 1881.

The writer wishes to express her grateful appreciation of the courtesy which, with generous promptitude, permitted the reproduction in English of a narrative so full, not only of edification, but of interest,— an interest heightened by the originality of character which distinguished the venerable subject of this memoir.

E. R.-B.

ARUNDEL.

Contents.

CHAP.	PAGE
I.—Early Years	13
II.—Professor and Prefect of Discipline	19
III.—Religious Vocation	36
IV.—Apostolate of the Prisons	44
V.—The Penitentiary of St. Sulpice. Ingenuity of his zeal in desperate cases	50
VI.—In the Pulpit	64
VII.—Traits of Popular Eloquence	75
VIII.—Action and influence upon Souls. The Crypt of St. Sulpice	84
IX.—Devotion to our Blessed Lady	94
X.—Devotion to Holy Church, and the Pope	103
XI.—The Society of St. Francis Xavier, and the "Holy Family"	109
XII.—Mingled Strength and Gentleness of Character. The Commune	117
XIII.—The Proscript. Last Days	126
XIV.—A Holy Death	133

FATHER MILLERIOT.

CHAPTER I.

Early Years.

ON the eleventh day of the present century, LOUIS ETIENNE MILLERIOT was born at Auxerre. The revolutionary tempest, which in the course of ten years had filled the land with ruins, had at last subsided, and France was beginning to breathe again. The churches, so long profaned, were restored to sacred uses, and the priests who had escaped death or returned from exile, were eagerly welcomed by the people, which had continued Christian, as it were, in spite of itself.

Thanks to the zeal of its clergy, and their fidelity to the traditions of its first bishops, one of the foremost towns to raise again its desolated altars was the ancient city of Auxerre. During the revolution all the parish priests of the city had, by their collective letter of the 13th of January, 1791, protested against the civil constitution; and when the persecution was over, they resumed their interrupted labours, seconded by the population, whose faith recent sufferings had strengthened and revived.

The parents of the young Louis were excellent Christians. God, however, often permits trials to those whom He loves; and during the troubles of their country they had suffered the loss of their fortune, so that it was in the stern school of hardship and privation that this child grew up who was destined to bear the name of his Master, and to suffer for Him.*

The tender affection for his family, of which his thoughtful and efficacious solicitude gave proof to the end of his life, was all the stronger because he had shared their difficulties from his earliest years. Besides, the succour of his parents was, in his eyes, the repayment of a debt,—a return for the

---

* Vas electionis est 'mihi iste, ut portet Nomen meum. ... Ego enim ostendam illi quanta oporteat eum pro Nomine meo pati. (*Act. Apost.* ix. 15, 16.)

hardy discipline of his training, as well as for his mother's gentler cares.

In accordance with a nearly-forgotten maxim, "*Qui aime bien châtie bien*,"—"He who loves well, chastises well,"—his father had been careful to correct his son's faults from a very early age, in such a manner as to impress upon his memory for life the immediate connection between fault and punishment.

When an old man, Father Milleriot would relate how, at the age of three, he brought upon himself a severe castigation for having repeated, without in the least understanding them, some impious expressions which had caught his ear in the street. "My father," he said, "heard me from the window, and immediately tapped at the pane, calling out sternly, 'What are you saying there, sir? *Come here!*' I thought myself dead then and there; my father, however, quickly made me feel that I was *not*."

But if his father impersonated justice, his mother, as we have implied, knew well how to temper justice with mercy; and God made use of her gentle influence to open the pure heart of her boy to the inspirations of His grace.

Father Milleriot has left the following account of the time of his First Communion, the event which was to determine all his future life.

"I did my best to prepare myself for this great act. Three months previously I read a book which, if it did me harm in some ways, yet in others did me much good, by giving a stamp of seriousness to my mind which lasted for years. This book was the *Instruction sur la Pénitence*, dedicated to the Duchesse de Longueville, and, as every one knows, full of Jansenist maxims. One day my mother found me in tears, with this book in my hand, and asked the cause of my trouble. I showed her some terrifying passages on the danger of profaning the Holy Eucharist, and told her how much I dreaded making a bad First Communion. 'My dear boy,' she answered, with her usual good sense, 'one cannot make a *bad* Communion when one really desires to make a *good* one.' I was comforted by her words, but still felt a latent fear which I could not get rid of, so that I was ready to make any sacrifice to avoid the danger I dreaded."

Nevertheless it was not long before love and trust overcame that excessive fear, which, because it is excessive, ceases to be "the beginning of wisdom." The child, like Samuel, listened without shrinking to the voice of his Heavenly Father calling him, and his heart answered simply and joyously, "Lord, here am I." For he tells us, as follows, how his vocation to the priesthood dated from this happy day. "My mother, before her marriage, had wished to enter the religious life, and, as if to compensate herself in some way for not having been allowed to carry out her wish, she said to me on the eve of my First Communion, 'My child, I have always heard that it is well on this great day to ask God to let us know our vocation. You will not forget to do this to-morrow morning?'

"I did not forget. When evening came, 'Well, Louis, did you think of what I said?'

"'Yes, mother.'

"'And what do you wish to be?'

"'Mother, I wish to be a priest.'

"My mother's joy may be imagined."*

The boy's prayer had indeed been granted. From that moment his resolution never once wavered, nor had he ever the least doubt as to his vocation.

* We mention once for all that the numerous quotations which will be found to occur in this book are all extracts from a MS. of Père Milleriot, of which the title is *Souvenirs d'un Vieux*.

CHAPTER II.

Professor and Prefect of Discipline.

THE revolution, besides profaning the churches, had closed the schools. In the matter of education, as in everything else, it had shown itself capable only of destruction, and powerless to build up the ruins it had made. Louis Milleriot found, therefore, none of those resources which the Church, when free, has always provided so abundantly for the sound education of youth, and God secured what was requisite for him by other means.

At the age of thirteen Louis had the good fortune to be taken into the house of an excellent priest, the Abbé Garnier, *Premier Vicaire* of his parish, and who instructed him in Latin. He showed the utmost eagerness and perseverance in study, and if permitted, would work from an early hour in the morning until night, without allowing

"My mother's joy may be imagined."

The boy's prayer had indeed been granted. From that moment his resolution never more wavered, nor had he ever the least doubt as to his vocation.

* We mention once for all that the numerous passages which will be found to occur in this book are all extracts from a MS. of Père Milleriot, of which the title is *Souvenirs d'un Pière*.

himself any recreation throughout the day. In the course of a year he had, pen in hand, translated the works of the chief Latin authors from beginning to end; he also wrote and spoke Latin with considerable facility.

This, however, was only a successful beginning. His parents, who were resolved at any cost to second the designs of Providence in regard to their son, sent him to Paris to complete his studies at the already flourishing institution founded, in 1804, by a generous and devoted priest, the Abbé Liautard.

This college, to which Louis XVIII. was to give one of his names,—that of Stanislas,—went at that time by the modest title of the "House of Education of *Notre Dame des Champs*," from the name of the street in which it stands. It began with five or six pupils, and in a few years had expanded so much as to form three large and distinct divisions, i.e., the *Petit Collège*, for the youngest; the *Collège* properly so called, for the bigger boys; and the *Seminaire de Notre Dame des Champs*, from whence issued several hundreds of priests and bishops, such as N.N.S.S. d'Héricourt, de Marguerie, Angebault, de la Tour d'Auvergne, &c., among the dead; and among the living, de Dreux-Brézé, de Briey, &c., &c.

Of his studious life in this Christian house there is no written record. What it must have been may easily be conjectured from the strong affection he ever after felt for his college, and also from the confidence reposed in him by his former masters,—a confidence shown by their recalling him soon after his departure to entrust him with important functions. When he had completed his studies, the director of the College Stanislas, M. Liautard, sent him, in the capacity of professor, to the *Petit Seminaire* of Châlons sur Marne; and, to sum up in a word the praises of his young protégé, wrote of him to M. Rollin, the superior, that he was "a man without guile." Father Milleriot, after two or three years at Châlons, was called to fill a similar post in the *Petit Seminaire* of Rheims.

The following incident recalls the words of Dr. Newman when, in his *Apologia*, he speaks of having had, as a youth, a vivid sense of "two, and two only, absolute and luminously self-evident beings, myself and my Creator."

Full of a lively faith, and in the habit of meditating on the great truths of eternity, which later on he was so earnestly to preach, the abbé was favoured in a manner very similar to that once experienced by St. Bruno in the same city. "A few moments after I had got into bed one night," (he wrote,) "I felt myself deeply impressed by the thought—always a most solemn one—of the soul appearing before God. Soon a profound terror took possession of me, and I trembled in every limb. Fearing lest I should die, I got up, hastened to my confessor, and told him my state of mind. Although not conscious of having committed any serious fault, I made my confession, and was absolved. Then, comforted and reassured, I went back to bed, and soon was quietly asleep. And," adds this humble priest, "what use did I make of this favour? Why did I close my eyes to this vivid light? God wished to make a saint of me, and it was only because I *would* not that He *could* not. When I must appear before Him to be judged, what shall I have to answer? Alas!

I shall be like the wicked servant in the Gospel, who had not a word to say. *At ille obmutuit.*"

From the *Petit Seminaire* of Rheims, Father Milleriot was sent for, to return to his beloved Collège Stanislas at Paris, and here remained for fifteen years as *Préfet de Discipline*. Kind and firm at the same time, he knew how to unite justice with charity, and although stern and inflexible in regard to serious misdemeanours, he dealt gently with mere boyish thoughtlessness and frolic. In 1828 the directorship of the *Petit Collège* was confided to him by the venerable M. Augé, Doctor of the Sorbonne, and formerly Vicar-General.*

The *Petit Collège* was, as we have said, composed of the younger and less advanced classes. Some of the old pupils take a pleasure in recalling the memory of those distant days, and of the young professor, "Monsieur Milleriot," who was looked up to by his boys with a feeling of filial fear, and whom M. Liautard had surnamed "The man of iron."

The Abbé Milleriot was, nevertheless, as much loved as he was feared. Though strictly a man of rule, he began by applying it rigorously to himself, in order to have a right to exact its faithful observance on the part of others. Moreover, in this he followed the bent of his mind, which was essentially methodical and orderly.

The first to rise and the last to rest, he presided over all the exercises between the class hours, and especially the various "*movements*" which precede and follow the hours of recreation,—critical moments, when silence is always more or less difficult to maintain; but a word or even a look from him sufficed to keep or restore order. The following anecdote will show how irresistible was his authority.

In the dusk of a winter's afternoon, the whole college was coming in after a long walk under the charge of a master against whom a general antipathy existed, and who was habitually accredited with the tastes and habits of a tyrant, possibly because he owned the name of Dionysius. In the course of the three or four hours' walk, he had been subjected to a series of tormenting annoyances which were but the prelude to a systematic revolt, plotted by the bigger boys, and which burst forth as soon as the school re-entered the college court. Here the demonstration began by shouts and cries, and the hoisting of a flag, intended to be tricolour, but formed, on the spur of the moment, of all the pocket-handkerchiefs and woollen comforters which came ready to hand. The bell rang for the classes to go in to study, but was drowned amid redoubled vociferations. The hapless Dionysius, "Master of studies," surrounded, taunted, threatened by a deafening crowd, knew not which way to turn, and in the obscurity vainly tried to identify the ringleaders of the tumult. Evening had come on, and for the first time probably the Abbé Milleriot was not there. The rioters, who thus had the field all to themselves, were loud in their shouts of triumph, when the door from the street into the court opened, showing against the dim twilight a tall dark figure, while a voice, which struck upon the rebels like a clap of thunder, uttered these simple words: "What is all this? Come! be quick! get into rank, and in silence!" It was like an avalanche on a house on fire; the whole was extinguished. Every one hurried into rank, the standard of revolt was abandoned on the field of battle, and when the reckoning time came with the morrow, the great anxiety was, *not* to recognize one's own handkerchief or necktie amid its complex formation.

The authority of Abbé Milleriot was absolute. Not a boy in the college would have either resisted or even attempted to dispute or discuss it. And this authority was not the result of any excessive severity, but rather of certain habits of discipline to which he had formed his pupils by training them in his own respect for the inviolability of the rule. He has sometimes been reproached with sacrificing feelings to regulations, and even of falling into an austere formalism which forbade a mutual confidence and openness between his pupils and himself. But this reproach was not merited. If there was little outward tenderness and freedom in his manner towards them, his heart was full of kindness and goodness to these boys, and this goodness revealed itself at times in a very touching manner. The following incident will serve as an example. A grave misdemeanour had been committed, and the culprit expelled. He had, however, declared that he had only acted at the request and under the compulsion of a schoolfellow in whose innocence Monsieur Milleriot had every reason to believe. This boy being sent for one evening to the Director's room, went, much disturbed at the unusual summons. The Abbé questioned him, with the severe countenance and unimpassioned coldness of a judge. The boy answered, but being naturally timid, as well as depressed by the sense of suspicion attaching to him, his replies lacked that unhesitating clearness and precision which, whether always justly or not, nevertheless carry conviction with them. At last, impelled by his anxiety to know the truth, and at the same time to establish the innocence of the boy in whom he felt an interest, the Abbé Milleriot yielded to the impulse of his heart, and took the only way to arrive at certainty. Throwing his arms affectionately round the lad, he spoke to him of his mother, whom he had lost, and of his father, who had only him, his young son, to be a comfort to him, and all this in a manner so compassionate and winning that the heart of the master won the heart of the boy, all barriers disappeared, and he was able to clear himself without difficulty.

When a man, he never forgot the delicate and tender kindness which had thus revealed in the somewhat dreaded Director a sensibility and power of sympathy with which people were not always disposed to accredit him.

It was about this time, and while still directing the *Petit Collège*, that Monsieur Milleriot was called upon to occupy himself particularly with a young man, whose edifying history he thus relates:

"The Abbé Augé, a holy man, if ever there were one, sent me a young man of twenty-four years of age to be educated with my little pupils. Once a cordwainer, and then a Trappist, he was thought by Dom Couturier, the abbot, to have a vocation for the ecclesiastical state. Nor was he mistaken, as will be seen, though at first sight the poor man had not much in his favour. Painfully plain, with rustic manners, and language to match, I must confess that my first impression on seeing him was one of decided dislike. However, I was not this time so crammed with self-conceit but that, by the grace of God, I overcame my repugnance, and forced myself to be kind to this poor fellow. Next day, when I went out with the boys, I made him walk with me, and it was then I learnt his history.

"Very soon I began to discover what treasures of the soul were concealed beneath that uninviting exterior, what innocence and purity, combined with a love of God, a zeal for souls, and a spirit of penitence truly admirable. From that moment I was vanquished. I took his instruction entirely into my own hands, taught him Latin (as best I could), and became his champion against my colleagues, who, not knowing him as I did, judged him, according to appearances, as a *minus habens,* incapable of entering the priesthood, and, to say the truth, my friends were very excusable in their opinion. Nevertheless, I persevered in my undertaking, and in time got my pupil into the *Grand Seminaire,* where he studied philosophy as well as he knew how, and theology after the same fashion. After being ordained priest, he was placed successively in three parishes, poor parishes in a poor diocese. There his zeal had free play. Easter communions soon increased tenfold; young people of eighteen to twenty-five made their first communion, and aged wanderers were brought back to love and practice their religion. When neighbouring curés would ask him how he managed to work some of these apparent miracles, he would answer simply, 'I only do what I can.' And this was indeed no small matter. His long and frequent watchings,—often whole nights,—were spent in prayer and in offering up his penances and austerities for the conversion of his dear parishioners. Knowing that he always wore a rough hair shirt, and regularly gave himself the discipline, I one day asked him how he could bear so much pain and constant discomfort. 'Oh!' he said, 'if only you knew how sweet these things are to me! And then I say to our dear Saviour, My Jesus, I offer this to You for the conversion of sinners.' Afterwards the Abbé Papin, (this was his name,) lived in Paris with his aged mother until the Crimean war broke out, when he went as an auxiliary chaplain to the army, and soon after died, a victim to cholera."

We will now resume our account in its

chronological order. When, in 1832, the cholera desolated Paris, the *Collège Stanislas* did not escape. In the class of philosophy only two scholars were left, who nevertheless valiantly maintained the honour of the rest by their successes at the *Concours Général*. It was at this time that, owing to a popular belief that the cholera was caused by the malicious poisoning of articles of food, and especially of water, one of those frightful acts of insane vengeance on the suspected, which not unfrequently occurred, was witnessed by Father Milleriot. "On the Place de Grève, the people, bewildered by rumours, were vociferating 'Death to the poisoners!' when two men began to fight, and after exchanging a few blows, one of them ran away. Immediately a voice shouted '*à l'Empoisonneur.*' It was his sentence of death. The people rushed upon him; in a moment he was covered with blood, and dragged along the ground to be thrown into the Seine, while some screamed 'Justice!' others 'Vengeance!' I can still see the unfortunate victim, frightfully disfigured and mutilated. . . . A minute afterwards and they were throwing him from the Pont d'Arcole. I was disguised; I contrived to get close to him, and gave him absolution."

In these moments of peril, Louis Milleriot already showed the calm and fearless energy of character which, in after years, distinguished him during the terrible days of the Commune.

About 1834, Father Milleriot was called to occupy the difficult post of Prefect of Discipline at the Great College. This title, without creating him new duties, appeared to render him somewhat more rigorous in the application of the rule. In having to deal with the more advanced youths who were now his charge, he felt himself on less smooth and more resistant ground. The wills were more decided, the characters more marked, the good and bad qualities of the man showed themselves with greater distinctness, and it needed more solicitude to repress the one and to develope the other. The vigilance of the new prefect grew in proportion to these exigences, and his intelligent activity knew no repose. Day and night he seemed everywhere at once, so impossible was it to escape his surveillance, which he exercised, moreover, after a fashion of his own.

Already, at the *Petit Collège*, M. Milleriot had accustomed himself to take a frequent part in the games with the boys. He continued to do the same with the young men, and the skill and agility, as well as heartiness, with which he joined in all their sports, made him a highly appreciated acquisition in the play-ground. He thus, in a certain sense, anticipated his entrance into the Company of Jesus, in whose houses of education the masters are in the habit of sharing in the games and recreations of their scholars. He prepared himself for it equally in his choice of the books out of which he gave the spiritual readings to the rhetoricians. Almost always it was Bourdaloue, whom he read and commented on with an elevation of views, an abundance of ideas, and an amount of practical wisdom, which gave a presentiment that he would one day shine as a spiritual director and in the pulpit. And yet at this time he never preached. He was content to explain the catechism or the Gospel soberly and even sometimes almost coldly, and when some one said, "But, Monsieur Milleriot, why do you not preach?" he answered, "I shall not preach before I am forty; until then will not be too long a time to prepare myself."

The resources of his mind may be imagined from the fact that when at the *Petit Collège*, during a long and rigorous winter, he every day improvised a new story, drawn entirely from his own imagination, for the benefit of the boys during their evening recreation in the refectory. In his tales of imaginary travels, for instance, he would relate one upon another the most burlesque and fanciful incidents and adventures, or the most unexpected predicaments, and so great was his power of interesting and captivating his young audience, that no recreation was considered complete without a story from Monsieur Milleriot.

But it was most particularly in his habits of daily life that the Abbé Milleriot forestalled his entrance into the life of the Society. Almost all his moments of liberty and leisure were spent in meditation and prayer, and, in order to secure undisturbed silence and recollectedness, he arranged for himself a humble oratory in an attic near his room. In this attic was an opening which looked into the chapel, and through this he could see the holy tabernacle.

His time and occupations were as methodically arranged as they were later on under the rule of St. Ignatius. In everything which regarded the material life he already observed a monastic austerity, often accepting or seeking all kinds of privations. Thus at the *Grand Collège*, when in charge of a *chambriste*, (the son of the Duc de Castries,) the pupil's room was never without a fire, but that of the master had scarcely one all through the intense cold of a severe winter.

The Abbé Milleriot remained only five or six years as Prefect of Discipline at the Great College. Possibly his government may have appeared too absolute for these elder youths, more independent than his former pupils, both as to age and ideas. In any case, after some difficulties which arose, the director of the college, M. Augé, thought well to ask him to return to the Little College. He did so with the simple humility of the true man of God, who knows how to obey, and recognizes the Divine Voice in that of his superior.

CHAPTER III.

Religious Vocation.

FOR more than twenty years Louis Milleriot had aspired to the religious life, and particularly to the Society of Jesus, but a succession of obstacles had impeded the accomplishment of his design. It was brought about at last by an unforeseen occurrence.

Having to find a substitute for a young *surveillant*, he went to see one of the Fathers in order to consult him as to a suitable person. "I was rising to take leave," he relates, "when, suddenly changing my mind, without having previously thought of it, or knowing exactly why or how, I opened my mind to him with regard to my desire to enter the Society, a desire of twenty-one years' standing, but which I was unable to satisfy." The Father listened very attentively, and promised to mention my wish to the Father Provincial. 'But,' I said, 'the superior of the *Collège Stanislas*, to whom I have already mentioned my project, considers that I have too strong a *will* of my own to be a Jesuit. For my own part, my will is to let myself be *ground* on entering the Company. But what do you think?' 'I think well of it,' he answered; 'it is men of your stamp who suit us.' A few days afterwards I saw the Father Provincial, the Rev. Père Guidée. He talked with me, questioned me, and inscribed my name to enter the noviciate at St. Acheul on the approaching vacation. 'But, *mon Père*, you do not know me.'—'I admit you.' And the matter was settled."

It was on the 10th of September, 1841, that the Abbé Milleriot, having bid adieu to the Collège Stanislas, set out for St. Acheul. He has left a rather amusing account of a small annoyance which happened as if to temper his great joy. He had made his sacrifice with all the gaiety and military *crânerie* which he put into everything, and had no idea of giving at the last moment any sign of weakness. The firmness of his courage, however, would scarcely have been unsuspected if judged from the appearance of his visage.

"On the way to St. Acheul," he says, "quite suddenly, and without any outward cause, a violent pain attacked my left eye; whether I owed it to a puff of wind or a blow from the demon I know not. In any case I had to enter and present myself to the Rev. Père Rubillon a piteous object, for my eyes were streaming with tears. According to custom, I was interrogated, and among other things Père Rubillon asked me, 'Is your health good?'

"'Splendid.'

"'Are you ever ill?'

"'Once in twenty-five years.'

"'Can you fast without difficulty?'

"'There is not a day on which I do not fast; but I would every day abstain from fasting if you were so to command me.'"

During the retreat for meditation and prayer, which all postulants are required to make before they are admitted into the noviciate, Louis Milleriot wrote the following statement of the motives of his present determination.

"MY CHOICE.

"In the sight of my God, and under the protection of His Blessed Mother, who is my Mother also, I, Louis Milleriot, priest unworthy, am resolved to make my choice and my election as here declared.

"Whom shall I choose for my portion, O my God, but Thee and Thee alone? Thee do I seek, but it is in the Company of Jesus that I desire to find Thee. My reasons are these:

"1. I perceive in this Company more abundant means than anywhere else to enable me to work out my own salvation and that of others. As a man and a Christian, I hunger after God; as a priest, I thirst to win souls to Him. Now, with the Jesuits, everything appears to me admirably to concur towards these two ends.

"2. Feeling myself particularly drawn towards preaching, and yet being conscious of the difficulties which have hitherto hindered me in regard to it, I believe that in the Company, more than anywhere else, I shall find facilities to this end, and for the conversion of souls, the sole aim to which I aspire.

"3. For more than twenty years I have desired to be a Jesuit. This desire has never varied, all my tastes and habits guiding me in the same direction. I believe, therefore, that this vocation comes from God, and I wish to follow it.

"4. Being exceedingly imperfect, and of great impetuosity of disposition, it seems to me that the Company offers me all the aids I need to enable me to correct my defects, and that probably it is there alone that I can hope for effectual amendment.

"These are my principal reasons for asking admission into the Company of Jesus.

"When I seek for reasons which might turn me from it, I cannot discover a single one. The difficulties which, according to nature, are attached to poverty and obedience have never appeared to me anything else than desirable. Nevertheless, should it be the will of God to subject me henceforth to a feeling of repugnance against them, I see in this only another means for my sanctification, and with the help of His grace I am resolved to accept and overcome it.

"In conclusion, I beg the Lord to bless my resolutions, and to enrich with His abundant favours the excellent superiors who are so kind as to trouble themselves about me. Amen."

God, who loves to try His own, saw fit to deprive His servant from that day forth of all the sensible consolations he had previously enjoyed. "Sensible devotion," so he wrote in his old age, "was cut off, as if with a razor, a few minutes before my entry into St. Acheul. I have continued dry and arid from that moment until now. Without doubt it is very much from my own fault, otherwise I would not complain. Before my noviciate I often felt a certain ardour in my love of God, the loss of which I have sometimes caught myself regretting. After some time spent in the noviciate, I one day said to the *Père Maître,* 'I am no longer now as I was before; I had then years of fervent devotion.' His answer I have never forgotten. 'Years of fervent devotion, precious without doubt. Years of sacrifice, a thousand times more precious.' Since this answer I have understood it all, at least in theory. In the Society one is taught to arm oneself in strength, not to exhale oneself in sweetness."

But, of those who in later years listened to Father Milleriot, who would have believed, had not he himself confessed it, that his greatest trial was to mount the pulpit? "What this cost me at first," he wrote, "and even for long afterwards, God only knows."

It is customary in the noviciate for the young men to practise themselves in little discourses, more or less improvised, or in the recitation of an oratorical formula, somewhat difficult because of the variety of gesture and intonation it implies. When Father Milleriot was required to make his first attempt, he tells us, "All was over with me now. I said to myself, 'I shall come to a dead stop. I shall faint, I shall fall. No matter; they will pick me up again. In any case into the pulpit I must mount.' And with this heroic act," he adds, "all my shyness vanished. Next day the *Père Maître* said, 'Then that cost you something?' 'Cost me something! —as much as if I had had to cut off my arm!'"

With regard to this lively apprehension, Father Milleriot writes a few lines which might almost be borrowed from the *Fioretti* of St. Francis of Assisi.

"One day, when on my way to the prison at Amiens, in company with a young Father who was also sent to preach in another part of the city, and who was scarcely less timid than myself, we heard the clucking of some hens, and I could not help exclaiming, 'Ah! those hens! if they only knew how happy they are! they have not got to preach!'"

A few years later Father Milleriot would have felt anything but happy if preaching had been forbidden him.

CHAPTER IV.

Apostolate of the Prisons.

WHILE yet a novice, Father Milleriot began the work which was to fill up the remainder of his long life. Liberty of Christian teaching did not exist in France, and the Jesuit Fathers, in order to be able to devote themselves to education, carried it on in exile, in Switzerland or Belgium. Thus, however flourishing their colleges at Brugelette or Fribourg might be, they only required a limited number of religious to carry them on. To this circumstance may probably be attributed the fact that Father Milleriot, who entered the Society at the age of forty-one, did not afterwards resume functions analogous to those which he had fulfilled at Châlons and at Rheims. Moreover, his superiors, in their carefulness to apportion to each individual member the duties best suited to his gifts, quickly perceived in Father Milleriot a wonderful aptitude for evangelizing the poor, and accordingly it was they who first allotted to him the lowly apostolate which was to earn for him the title of *Le Ravignan des Ouvriers,*—the Ravignan of the working-men.

He was sent to make his first trial of arms in the prisons. With what effect may in some small measure be gathered from his diary.

"I was visiting the prison in one of our large cities, in company with one of the Fathers, and observed in the courtyard a convict in a red garment, and with his feet chained. 'Oh,' I thought, 'here is some prey worth catching!' and I went up to the man.

"'My friend, where do you come from?'

"'Toulon.'

"'What is your sentence?'

"'The galleys, for life.'

"'Why?'

"'Helping in a murder.'

"'Are you married?'

"'Yes.'

"'Where is your wife?'

"'In jail for theft.'

"'Have you children?'

"'Four.'

"These dry, short answers may be imagined, but not the ferocious expression of the man's eyes, which were those of a wild beast. When I tried to induce him to make his peace with God, his reply was too blasphemous to repeat. We began a novena for his conversion at the same time that we were giving the retreat, and after it was ended I returned to the prison.

"'Now, my friend, you will make your confession?'

"'I am quite willing.'

"And on the following morning, he, with twenty more of the prisoners whom we had brought back to God, received Holy Communion. The curé of the parish, who came for the close of our retreat, said to us afterwards, 'Who is that convict in red, to whom I gave Holy Communion this morning? I was struck with the remarkable gentleness of his countenance. I never saw any one receive the Sacred Host with greater devotion.'"

Again, "One of the Fathers and myself were giving a retreat in a prison. A woman came to confession, and I afterwards gave her the scapular, making her promise always to wear it. A fortnight afterwards, on returning to the prison, I found this woman in the court.

"'Well, mother, how are we getting on?'

"'Ah, since I have not seen you, father, I have been getting on very badly indeed.'

"'What has happened?'

"'Why, father, since I have not seen you, I have been and hung myself.'

"'Hung yourself, my poor child? What, (and I smiled,) hung yourself by the neck?'

"'Yes, father, by the neck. Ah, if you only knew how it hurts one!'

"'Well, tell me all about it.'

"'Why it was just this. For a little theft, a mere trifle, you know, I got a month of detention. When it was over, and as soon as I had made my confession, I went back to my companions, and found them accusing me of something infamous. 'What!' I said, '*I* capable of such a thing? You are a set of abominable creatures!' And then, in despair, I ran to throw myself into the well in the court, but they held me back. 'Never mind,' I said, 'since you accuse me as you do, I shall finish myself somehow.' And as soon as I got the chance, I went up to the garret, and hung myself from a large nail. I was already choking when I thought of my scapular, and lifted my heart to the Blessed Virgin. That moment the rope broke, and I fell on my feet. True, father. *What a God God is!*'

"'Well, my daughter, you owe a beautiful taper to our Blessed Lady,' I said. The poor woman was cured of the wish to finish herself."

This was in 1841. The next year we find Father Milleriot at Notre Dame de Liesse, where he went to finish his noviciate. From this time, until October, 1843, his life was one of continual movement throughout the dioceses of Soissons and Beauvais. After two missions given, the one at Ergny, the other at Aquin, he wrote in his *Journal de ses Ministères*, "heard two thousand five hundred confessions." This was pretty well for a novice.

The following is one little episode of this successful apostolate mentioned in his diary. "I was sent to preach a mission in the country. A young man met me to carry my bag. I gave him the miraculous medal for himself, and one for each of his three brothers, getting him to promise that they would all wear it.

The mission began. In the evening the young man came to ask me to hear his confession, adding, 'Ever since this morning your medal seems to say to me without ceasing, ' *Va te confesser! va te confesser!*'

"'That is well; but, my friend, you must bring me your brothers.'

"'I will try.'

"A second and a third were faithful to the rendezvous, but the fourth, proving somewhat restive, his brothers brought him and pushed him into the confessional. 'Here's the fourth, father. Now *you* must look after him.' The task was by no means difficult. It was a case of *le premier pas qui coûte*, and by the time the youth left the confessional, he was very glad to have entered it, even against his will."

CHAPTER V.

The Penitentiary of St. Sulpice. Ingenuity of his zeal in desperate cases.

FROM the time of his arrival in Paris, Father Milleriot, without neglecting any of the duties, interior or exterior, of his vocation, attached himself most especially to the ministry of reconciliation in the confessional. Affable and good to all, he had a particular "weakness" for the very poorest and the most repulsive. His more habitual and preferred clients were men, and among these the ignorant, the laggards as to their religious duties, the great sinners. To draw into his net "big fish" of this description, as he would smilingly call them, was the joy of his heart.

The following was the day's work of this Grand Penitentiary of St. Sulpice, unvarying in its regularity, and faithfully observed up to the eve of his death. He rose at three instead of four, in order to have another hour to give to God. This exception to the ordinary rule he was careful to have periodically authorized by his superior. After his meditation, he said his Mass, a little before five o'clock; then followed his thanksgiving, and after this his slender breakfast,—a cup of coffee and a morsel of bread,—which he took standing. At half-past six, with the firm and martial step which characterized his walk, he started for St. Sulpice, and established himself in his confessional, surrounded by medals, scapulars, rosaries, sacred pictures, and little books, which he was in the habit of giving to his "children."

About half-past ten he returned to his cell in the rue de Sèvres, from whence, several times in the week, he would again set out to continue his fatiguing ministry through the whole of the afternoon. The rest of the day was spent in the recitation of the Breviary, and in preparing his addresses and instructions, the notes for which were carefully written on small leaflets all of one size. This life of toil he led joyfully for more than thirty-six years.

As may readily be supposed, his memory

was enriched with many a tale of interest and edification; but, with the great discretion which befits a confidant of souls, he never related any without having first obtained express permission from the persons whom it concerned. Thus, when in his *Souvenirs* he happens to mention a proper name, he is careful to add, "I am authorized by so-and-so to mention his name, in order to give a fuller authenticity to my account." This was the case with one whom Father Milleriot calls "*mon vieux Jeannin*," and whose story he heads with the significant title of

"A DESPERATE CASE.

"The father of one of our working-men belonging to the Society of St. Vincent de Paul, and who was eighty-six years of age, was afflicted with a nervous affection of long standing. When I asked after him, the son spoke of his father as having no religion.

"'I am glad to know this,' I said. 'The first time I meet him, I will give him a good shake of the hand.'

"'Ah, Father, don't trust to that; you

may be certain that he will say something rude to you.'

"'Very well, we will see.'

"Not long after, my man suddenly finds himself face to face with me. '*Bonjour, Monsieur Jeannin,*' I said, taking his hand, 'how is it with you to-day?'

"Starting back violently, he exclaimed, 'I have no love for priests.'

"'Well, if you have no love for priests, I *have* love for people who speak their mind frankly, as you do; besides, if you do not love priests, you love the good God.'

"'Leave me alone, will you, with your good God?'

"'*With all that,* you can easily say a little bit of a prayer morning and night.'

"'Leave me in peace, with your —— prayers.'

"'Adieu, Monsieur Jeannin, *à l'occasion.*'

"He was trembling with rage.

"'Well, *coquin,*' I thought, (addressing myself,) 'you shall pay for the others. My God, come to my aid! Often You have given me the grace to carry a soul by storm at the first or second encounter. This one I will lay siege to for as long a time as shall be necessary.' I resolved to take my old man by his mouth. By one of my penitents I sent him a good meat pie and two bottles of wine. This charitable person presented herself, and began, 'Monsieur Jeannin, Father Milleriot sends you a pâté for yourself and your son, with two bottles of wine to drink his health.' The old man, furious at first on hearing my name, quickly calmed down. 'Madame—pray be seated......Father Milleriot......is very good.' This was something. Not long afterwards I went to his house. 'M. Jeannin, it is your friend come to see you.' 'Reverend Father, will you take a seat?' This was better still; but we were as yet far from anything like business. It was necessary to reiterate at regular intervals the envoy of the pie and the bottles. I went every month to see him, and every month I gained ground.

"We had few discussions. I preferred to win him by his heart. By degrees he began of his own accord to pray. Then at each visit we said together the *Our Father* and *Hail Mary*. At last, after four years of waiting, he was won. He made his confession, and I gave him his Easter Communion in his room, which he had not for a long time been able to leave. Before his Communion he asked me to let him say a word to his son in my presence. It was this: 'Listen, Jacques. Your old father is going to renew his First Communion, made seventy-nine years ago. You also are behindhand with your duties. You are free, but if you think well, do the same as I.' He then with great piety received the Most Holy Sacrament. Six months later he was dying. I gave him myself the last sacraments of the Church, and he quietly departed, at the age of ninety-two."

God had long waited for this soul,—a soul, it may be, more unfortunate than guilty. His priest, wise and loving, careful to take the divine patience as the model for his own, thus had the joy, after four years of delicate solicitude, of bringing the wanderer home.

The next is a rather similar case.

A Sister of St. Vincent de Paul had, for months, visited a sick woman who could not make up her mind to confess. An excuse was always ready. Sometimes she was too ill to receive the last sacraments, sometimes not ill enough, and then it was too much trouble in her weak state, or she would not know how to begin, and so on. The real obstacle, however, was her husband, who would not suffer a priest even to be mentioned, lest it might give his wife "her deathblow," and declared that should one show himself, he would shut the door in his face.

At last the woman, feeling that her end was near, told the sister her wish to see a priest, at the same time asking her to "find one who is old and kind."

"I know one who will suit you," was the answer; "the father of the working people."

Thereupon she went for Father Milleriot, but although preparing him to find the husband the reverse of accommodating, she omitted to mention that he was the *concierge*,—the porter of the house. We continue the account from the Father's journal.

"I present myself to the *concierge*. 'Does Madame X. live here?'

"'She does; she is my wife. What do you want with her?'

"'Your wife, my good man? Ah, I did not know that. I am told that she wishes to see me.'

"'And *I* tell you that see her you will *not;* so make haste to be off!'

"'Certainly, my friend. I am not come here to force myself into any one's house, and I will not see your wife without your permission.' So saying, I put on my hat as if to go, but turned again. 'My friend, I perceive that you have a heart, and that you dearly love your wife.'

"'Love her? I believe so.'

"'I knew it; and that you would not willingly cause her any pain.'

"'Certainly not.'

"'On the contrary, you would be very glad to give her pleasure.'

"'Of course; no need to say that.'

"Then, turning to the sick woman, 'And you too, good mother, I am sure you love your husband very dearly?'

"'Oh yes, Monsieur le curé, indeed I do; my man is the best of men!'

"'Worthy, excellent people! *This* is what I call speaking out; *this* is what I call a happy couple! Well, my children, I am so pleased with you, that I will pray the good God to restore health to the sick one. Come, my friend, let me say a *Pater* and *Ave* by her side, to ask that she may get better.' And the man let me do as I liked.

"'Well, mother, now don't you feel a little more comfortable?'

"'Yes, Monsieur le curé.'

"'And won't you let me say a little word of consolation to you?'

"'Very willingly.'

"Then to the husband, 'My good friend, leave me for a few moments with your wife, that I may say a few good words to her.' And without waiting for his reply, I took him by the shoulders, and put him very gently out of the room. Needless to say that the 'consolation' for the sick woman was a regular confession, as short as possible on account of her imminent danger. As soon as the matter was ended, I fetched the good man in, and bade him ask his wife if she was not happy.

"Quite happy,' she said.

"'Well, my children, see how well we have got on! Now, father, give me pen and ink; I am going to write the note for the sacraments.'

"'Wife, is it true?'

"'Yes.'

"The poor man was pale with emotion, but did not attempt to make any resistance, and almost immediately the administration of the last sacraments took place. When I returned on the morrow, the woman was still living, but she died the following day. Two days after I went to express my sympathy to the poor man. 'My friend, your wife has set you a good example, and saved her soul. You must follow it if you would some day join her in heaven. Do as she did; come to me one of these days; we will arrange our little affairs together.' 'I see it plainly,' he answered; 'yes, I must end by that.' I embraced him affectionately. My indomitable *concierge* was conquered."

At the confessional in St. Sulpice, in which Father Milleriot daily spent so many hours, strange penitents sometimes presented themselves.

One day, a workman entered the church, and asked the verger to tell him of any priest who "for three francs" would give him the note or ticket of confession necessary for his marriage! Refusing to accept his assurance that the thing was impossible, that it was not a matter of payment, but that before a priest could give the required note he must have heard the confession, the man began to argue and insist. Father Milleriot, attracted by the noise, left the confessional, and after learning the cause of this singular discussion, took possession of the angry man, saying, cheerfully, "Come, my friend, I can settle your affair." He talked to him kindly, gave him medals for himself and his future wife, and when he had secured his good graces, he gradually instructed him, showing him the greatness of the sacrament of penance, heard his confession, and gave him, needless to say *gratis,* a good absolution.

Another time, a man of the people walked straight up to Father Milleriot, went down on one knee, and told him he was going to be married next day. As for his confession, that, he said, was soon made. "I have nothing at all to say to you, monsieur, except that *there is nothing that I have not done.* There!"

"You have done everything, my friend?"

"Yes, monsieur, I have."

"Have you killed the Pope?"

"Oh, no."

"Well then, my good man, you make yourself out to be worse than you are. Come, go in there; kneel down well on both knees, then I will make you my little wedding present, and all will be right; you will be pleased with me, and I shall be pleased with you." And thus the affair was satisfactorily arranged.

Father Milleriot was especially at home with military men. He loved their frankness, and their confidence was quickly gained by his own.

An officer one day came to thank him for the attentions he had shown his wife throughout her last illness.

"And now, general, it is your turn."

"Father, I do not go to confession."

"I know that; but it is a thing which must be done."

"Father, I beg to repeat that I do *not* confess."

"No, general, you do not, but you will."

And the old officer, gradually subjugated by the ascendancy of this energetic and holy priest, answered, half smiling, the questions he went on to ask him.

"Now, general, you have made your confession in jest, but you will come back and make it in earnest."

And he did in fact afterwards return of his

own accord, and after three visits, his confession being ended and his absolution received, great indeed was his joy.

"I was sure of you all along," said the father.

"And why, if you please?"

"Because for ten years you have worn the miraculous medal."

These generous conversions were the consolation and reward of this apostolic heart; but it had its trials also. Several times in the diary occurs the memorandum, "Father Milleriot well caught;" or "Father Milleriot finely cheated." One pretended penitent steals his breviary, another his old umbrella, or a false *dévote* disappears with his spectacle case or his handkerchief. Sometimes he caught the culprit in the very act, and then, after rebuking him or her soundly, he would end by giving the thief an alms. "For after all," he would say, "it is their destitution which drives these poor people to steal." And thus he suffered his kind heart to over-rule his prudence. He sometimes, however, made it a subject of self-reproach that he had grown a little mistrustful, and even, so *he* judged, even a little hard. This was the case when, for instance, an importunate beggar would come and say, "Father, if you don't assist me I shall go and drown myself, or blow out my brains." And then the father contented himself with answering, with his kindly smile, "My friend, out of ten who kill themselves in this fashion, there is not one that dies of it."

One day Father Milleriot had to appear as a witness at the assizes, an unhappy woman, fallen from an honourable position into misery and sin, having thought proper to appeal to the kind father to say a word in her behalf. Being questioned by the president, Father Milleriot simply answered, as might have been with certainty foreseen, "I declare that in my quality of confessor to the accused, I have nothing to say either for her or against her."

CHAPTER VI.

In the Pulpit.

IF Father Milleriot in his dealing with souls had a special predilection for the confessional, this did not by any means lead him to neglect the public ministry of the pulpit.

The characteristics of his eloquence are not easy to describe. It was remarkable for its originality, being peculiarly his own, and resembling that of no one else. After a pastoral retreat preached by him at Orleans, Mgr. Dupanloup could not refrain from saying to him, "Father, you are truly eloquent."

"Monseigneur," answered the father, "my powers expand with my audience, most particularly when I am addressing priests. *Then* there are, for me, no more hearers, no more preachers, (pardon me, my lord,) no more bishops; there is only truth itself."

When, in 1854, he was preaching, at St.

Thomas d'Aquin, a retreat preparatory to the paschal communion, the church was filled every evening by men of the people, for whom these instructions were more particularly intended.

"But do you know, Father," said the venerable curé, "that among your audience you have marchionesses, duchesses, and other distinguished people of the highest rank?"

"Well, then, to-morrow these noble personages shall have a little word to their own especial address."

Next day, therefore, the discourse began as follows:

"My brethren, I am the man of the people, and it is my joy to be so. I prefer preaching the Gospel to the little rather than the great, and to confess the poor rather than the rich, domestics and artizans more than the masters and the nobles. Not that I despise the noble; on the contrary, no one can honour them more than I, especially when, like those who hear me, they are more noble in heart than even in name, more distinguished for their religion than for their titles. Moreover, to give them a proof of my devotedness, and thus induce them to grant me their confidence,

I will add in all simplicity that, without the slightest embarrassment I would receive in my confessional the Pope on one side and the Emperor on the other."

A smile, which the hearers could not repress, showed that they comprehended the invitation, and the remaining days of the retreat showed that they accepted it, from the numerous men and women of the world who flocked to St. Sulpice to confess to Father Milleriot.

A few years later, (1865,) he was preaching the Lent at Notre Dame des Victoires. Before one of his sermons, when raising his hand to make the sign of the Cross, he suddenly stopped, looked round upon the congregation, and in his grave and deep voice exclaimed, "How grand a thing it is, my brethren, thus to offer and consecrate our actions to our Father who is in heaven, to our Lord Jesus Christ who has ransomed us, to the Holy Ghost who is unceasingly with us to sanctify us! How grand a thing is the sign of the Cross! Do you make it well? Let us try together,—*In Nomine Patris, et Filii, et Spiritus Sancti;*"—and at the same time he made upon himself a large sign of the

Cross, all present, much moved, following his example.

On another occasion he was speaking of the sad fate of sinners, and quoted the words of the holy Curé d'Ars, "*They are too unfortunate!*" At this moment he turned towards the entrance of the church, where some men were standing, and exclaimed, "Ah, yes! poor sinners! they are too unfortunate! On your knees, sinners; we will pray for you." And falling on his knees in the pulpit, he continued, in a voice of earnest solemnity and pathos, "For the sinners,—men and women,—for all who are far from God, but who are about to return to Him, to be converted, to confess their sins, let us pray for them. 'Remember, O most sweet Virgin Mary;'" and with the deepest fervour and emotion he recited the *Memorare* for their intention.

M. Fournel, an able writer under the *non de plume* of Bernadille, took Father Milleriot as the subject of one of his literary notices in the *Français*,* and we take the liberty of quoting some passages from his sketch.

* 30 March, 1877.

"Do you know the Church of St. François Xavier? Scarcely. It is a long way off, not far from the Invalides: it is an edifice of new Paris, of an architectural arrangement not easy to describe, but combining in itself something of the antique, the romantic, and the renaissance all at once, and, in spite of all this, by no means ugly.

"One Sunday evening I was passing that way. In the sombre depth of the boulevard I saw the vague outline of the façade, capped by its two towers. The distant sound of the organ attracted me, and I went in.

"The organ ceased. A white-headed priest with well-marked features ascended the pulpit, as I took my seat in the midst of a congregation consisting, by far the most part, of 'the people.'

"The perfect ease of the preacher's manner denoted long habit. He was evidently quite at home. He began in a voice which, without the least effort, filled the church. He preached about prayer, and painted in picturesque and effective touches the smallness of man with regard to God, his miseries, his needs, and then the lawfulness, the use, and the necessity of prayer.

"As he went on, he answered those philosophers (falsely so-called) who, on the one hand, affirm that prayer is useless, and, on the other, that it is a slight offered to the goodness and justice of God, who knows our wants without our telling Him. And his answer, free as it was from abstract metaphysics, dealt a blow none the less telling, at this false philosophy. Lofty and familiar, winning and commanding by turns, but always vivid, original, full of sparkling and unexpected sallies, he kept the attention fully awake, and the mind and heart fully interested. With a facility and variety that would have disconcerted Bourdaloue, he passed from grave to gay, from gentle to severe. Comparisons and metaphors seemed to spring up spontaneously as he went on. He would bring himself familiarly upon the scene, relate his experiences, appeal to the curé of the parish, tell some anecdote or story with an imitative voice and gesture which delighted his audience. Then, seizing the rein with a firm hand, he would stir the soul, touch the heart, dominate the mind, carry his hearers with him, as if into the Divine Presence, up into the very light of the Face of God. One thing was certain, that never for a moment would they think of going to sleep.

"I had never heard such preaching as this. The nearest to it in freedom, abruptness, and vigour, was that of the Abbé Combalot, but this resemblance was only partial.

"'Who is this priest?' I asked my neighbour, a solidly built young carpenter or mason apparently, and who had listened with all his might.

"He looked at me in unfeigned surprise.

"'*Who?* why, it is Father Milleriot.'

"This told me all. I had often heard of Father Milleriot, but had never seen him until then. The *Ravignan des Ouvriers* is not in the habit of preaching in educated parishes, but delights in the uncultured population of outlying regions. There, with strong hand, this 'fisher of men' draws into his net abundant prey, if such an expression be permissible as the 'prey' of salvation. But in truth his homely and forcible eloquence is well calculated to drive conviction into the hardest heads, and take the most rebellious hearts by storm, and compel them to surrender.

"Returning home, I opened my directory, but although I found in it a crowd of *Mes-*

sieurs whom I never heard of, I did not find Father Milleriot. It was necessary therefore to inquire elsewhere. Not of *himself*, by any means. He is never visible except in the pulpit, or by some sick bed, or in his confessional at St. Sulpice; and I have a suspicion that the rash journalist who should venture to ask him for particulars about himself would be summarily sent about his business, or, more likely still, would be invited then and there to go down 'upon his knees and make his confession, a possibility which the said journalist might be shy of risking.

"Father Milleriot is seventy-eight years of age. 'I am quite aware,' he would say, 'that I am somewhat *elderly*, but I am not *old*.' And he is right. No one who knows him well ever thinks of looking upon him as an old man. Not only has he kept all his gaiety and cheerfulness of spirit and his powerful voice, but also all the activity, ardour, and energy of early manhood. He is the very man for evangelizing the savages of civilization, and in particular the Red-men of Paris.

"'A Jesuit, that one?' inquired one workman of another, after hearing Father Milleriot.

"'Yes, a Jesuit, you innocent! Don't you

know that the Jesuits are the pick of all that is first-rate among the priests?'

"This was the answer; but I can well understand the astonishment of the questioner, considering what is sometimes pretended, namely, that Jesuits all resemble one another, like so many soldiers; never indulge in a gesture which is not pre-arranged by their Rule, and only hold their heads, raise their hands, or lower their voices, except as prescribed and determined in the Spiritual Exercises of St. Ignatius. We must therefore suppose that Father Milleriot had either never been properly run into shape, or else that he had broken the mould."

The lively journalist is mistaken. Father Milleriot had not "broken the mould." Never did the idea occur to St. Ignatius of effacing in his religious any personal originality or characteristic in favour of I know not what automatic uniformity. His Rule aims at repairing, within as well as without, that which is defective, and probably no one more determinedly endeavoured to conform himself to this Rule than did Father Milleriot, but he did not for this reason lose or suppress his special turn of mind, his vivid and graphic language, nor his easy, joyous, and martial bearing.

M. Fournel, as we have seen, compared Father Milleriot to the celebrated Abbé Combalot, and not without reason. Thus, when the abbé died like a soldier at his post, in the middle of the Lenten retreat he was preaching at St. Roch, Father Milleriot was at once thought of as fittest to continue the retreat thus sorrowfully interrupted.

His first sermon on this occasion made a deep impression. It was on Hell. He proved its existence and described its horrors. Then announcing the next conference, he undertook to prove with no less certainty that after all *hell need not exist.* "And," he added, "I invite you, mesdames, to bring your husbands with you. They cannot fail to be gratified by the subject of which I give notice."

Accordingly the next conference was crowded, and very numerously by men. The father began with the words of our Blessed Lord: "All power is given to Me in heaven and in earth. Whatsoever you shall loose on earth, shall be loosed in heaven." Then, dwelling on a thought which was habitual to him, he insisted on this verity, that each one for himself, by the grace of the sacrament of penance, can close hell, and cause, in fact, that for him hell shall not exist. "Confess, therefore, my dear brethren, confess your sins, for in the merciful designs of Jesus Christ a good confession suppresses hell."

CHAPTER VII.

Traits of Popular Eloquence.

ONE reason of the delight the people took in their favourite preacher, and one great secret of his success, lay in the fact that, without ever descending to triviality, Father Milleriot spoke to them in their own simple and forcible language, abounding in imagery and telling comparisons. Avoiding whatever was beyond the range of the ordinary apprehension, he made it his aim, before all else, to be clearly understood, and, while informing the mind, to move and win the heart to good. We will quote a few examples of his usual style, which, if it could not be regarded as a *chef d'œuvre* in a literary point of view, was at least never tedious, the worst fault of style possible for the pulpit orator, as for any other.

"One day I was assisting at the Benediction of the Blessed Sacrament, and while listening in the silence of my soul to the harmonies of the organ, I said to myself, 'Would that I possessed as powerful a voice! I would seek out the largest churches, I would mount the pulpits, and say, 'Listen, my brethren, to the verities of the faith.' Much more, I would that my voice had the power of thunder, to sound in the ears of men these tremendous words, 'Whither are you going, O ye senseless ones? Do you not see hell open beneath your feet?' I would arouse them with the terrible cry of 'Fire! Fire!' Yes, to the fire with the impious, the blasphemers, the impure! To the fire with those respectable people in the eyes of the world, who live in the world as if there were no God.'

"Never, you think, will such a voice come to disturb the peace of our cities. Ignorant that you are! You will one day hear this formidable voice, or rather a voice more formidable still. Deny it not, I beseech you. Remember what the Gospel tells you of the last days, when the trumpet shall sound to the ends of the world, *Surgite mortui*—Arise, ye dead, and come to judgment.

"Hear another voice, the voice of the Son of Man. Son of Man, speak. The damned, the milliards of the damned will hear: 'Go ye into everlasting fire, you who have shut your ears to the gentle voice of the Lamb when He spoke to your hearts.' But this Lamb is become the Lion of Judah, at whose roar the universe shall shake. And *then* you would repent. It will be too late!

"But as yet there is time. Listen to the voice of the priest; cry to the God of mercy. The voice of repentance shall drown the voice of justice. Come to the sacred tribunal, there you will confess your faults, there you will pour forth your prayers and tears, there you will receive the pardon of your sins, and with pardon you will also find peace for your hearts, and rest for your troubled souls."

When Father Milleriot took possession of an idea or a word, he would turn them in all directions, and even from this repetition itself would produce great effects.

"How fearful a catastrophe is an earthquake! In that of Lisbon, only a century ago, fifty thousand persons perished. In that of Constantinople, at an earlier date, five hundred thousand met their death. Well, still more terrible are the shocks of the demon. The Gospel shows him to us as a terrible winnower, seeking to winnow the elect, and cast them into the abyss. But the shocks of the demon are nothing to the shocks of God, if one may venture to say so. God shakes the tree that the bad fruit may fall off from it. He also shakes the tree planted by the waters, that He may cause it to take deeper root, and bring forth better fruit, and more abundantly.

"There will be a final shock from God at the end of time. God will grasp the earth by its two poles, and shake off the impious from it. Let us, then, (still to take the same image,) let us shake off our softness, our evil habits, our unbridled passions. Ah, we should do this did we only at each striking of the clock, at each sound of earth, listen to the monotonous and ceaseless stroke of the pendulum of eternity, which seems to say, 'For ever! for ever! for ever!'"

Once more; how could a speaker fail to establish a mutual communication between himself and his hearers, whose discourse opened thus:

"Can you read? Yes. You are fortunate. I wish I could. All the same, you do *not* know how to read. You read books written in ink by the hand of men, but how about the great book of Christians, the book written by the Hand of God, in the Blood of God, the crucifix? The peasants sometimes say, 'How learned he is! he reads big books!' But who reads the great book of all? Almost no one."

Sometimes, in seeking the confidence of his hearers, Father Milleriot would comment, in his own fashion, on the words of our Lord to His apostles, "I will make you fishers of men."

"If a fisherman found in his net a half drowned man, what would not be his joy to bring him to life again! Well, this is the joy of the confessor, the preacher, the priest. Come, then, suffer yourselves to be taken in our nets; we will give you to God our Master, we will not *sell* you. It is Jesus Christ our Lord who sold Himself for you. Come, then, we will not *eat* you; we invite *you* to eat the Bread of heaven. And again, the larger the fish, the better pleased is the fisherman. To the confessor, the fine fish is the man who is twenty years behindhand with his duties,—a pike of twenty pounds; or the woman ten years in arrears with hers,—a carp of ten pounds."

Then, having gained in this way the full attention of his hearers, Father Milleriot went on to give them practical advice, or would explain to them the plan they were to follow in order to make a good confession. Here again familiar examples abounded. For instance: "Look at my cassock; it is buttoned awry, and wants doing over again. It is just the same with an ill-made confession; it must be done over again; you must *re-unbutton* your conscience before you can make it right."

Our Divine Saviour, in preaching the Gospel to little ones and the poor, was pleased to speak to them in parables. Faithful to this great example, Father Milleriot was in the frequent habit of clothing the verities of the faith in the attractive garb of a story, and in this he would sometimes boldly improvise himself as the hero.

The following is somewhat abridged:—"I had a dream. I was a merchant, and, throwing myself into great commercial enterprises, I made fifty per cent. or a hundred thousand francs of profit every day. I had no losses; it was charming. Well, in ten years—(I always rested on Sundays and holidays)—I should have gained three hundred millions of francs, or an income of fifteen millions.

"And yet in my dream I desired something more. Riches did not satisfy me. It seemed as if there were *a hole in my heart* which nothing would fill up.

"I took to oratory, and as an orator became incomparable. All the world ran to hear me. Demosthenes, Bossuet, O'Connell, were mere children compared to me. Alas! there was still that *hole in my heart.*

"I wished for royalty, and became a king, the greatest that ever was. At my first telegram all other kings hurried to my capital. I thought that now I should be happy. No, I was not. Nothing filled *that hole.*

"And in my dream I called to me all the pleasures of the world, and they came in crowds; I swam in an ocean of delights. But what were they? All were nothingness, misery, and pain.

"As in my sleep I preserved deep sentiments of faith, I asked God to let me taste all the sweetness of His grace and the favour of His love. God heard me, and I drank freely of all the celestial consolations with which at times the souls of the saints are inundated.

ght, a cer-
penetrated.
his desires,
al of hap-

is superior
olutionary
f personal
; "a little
prison, un

his diary,
rds, which
I was not
t troubles.
l to God's
me to join

Oh, what an unspeakable difference! All the pleasures of life were utterly contemptible compared with these torrents of joy. *Then,* without doubt, I was at the summit of happiness. No, not yet.

"Something told me that the greatest grace which God grants to a soul is the *love of suffering;* that in this world the greatest happiness is to suffer for the love of God. And it seemed in my dream that I was martyred. Like another Ignatius of Antioch, I was about to be thrown to wild beasts......I saw myself suffering death, and flying straight to heaven......It was too much happiness, too great joy for my weakness to bear. I awoke.

"What do you think of this? Ah, dream, dream an ideal happiness as perfect as you may, you will never reach the height of good which God has in store for His own. You are too great, your heart is too vast, for its immense capacity to be filled by anything, by everything, except by God."

This, if we mistake not, is in itself very fine, but that which sent home these powerful words was the profound earnestness and conviction of the heart from which they sprang. Thus, what Father Milleriot called a *dream,* was to him an ever-present thought, a certainty with which his heart was penetrated. He had made the offering of all his desires, and this was truly, to him, the ideal of happiness.

At the period of the commune, his superior asked him if he regarded these revolutionary disturbances with any feeling of personal anxiety. "No, Father," he replied; "a little prison, a little death,—*un peu de prison, un peu de mort,*—does one good."

"And," he adds humbly in his diary, "these alas! were nothing but words, which lost themselves in emptiness, and I was not found worthy to perish in our recent troubles. Perhaps, had I been less unfaithful to God's favours, He might have suffered me to join our martyrs."

CHAPTER VIII.

Action and Influence upon Souls.—The Crypt of St. Sulpice.

"FATHER MILLERIOT," wrote the Abbé Mullois, in his *Cours d'Eloquence Populaire*, "is entirely devoted to the working classes and the poor. To them he gives up everything, his time, his strength, his preaching, his heart, and his life. But in order to appreciate what this means, one must see him in the midst of his dear people, an auditory which would frighten many an ordinary man, but with whom he is as happy as a father surrounded by his children. Above all, one must *hear* him. His people express what they feel about him in a very graphic manner. 'No chance of holding out,' said one; 'he thrusts his words into your body in spite of you.' Father Milleriot goes straight to the point,—confession and conversion. Sinners on their knees like little children, and praying to their Father who is in heaven,—these are the trophies of his devotion. He has a special attraction to the bad, and if they have a touch of the scoundrel about them, well, the greater the rejoicing in heaven when they are brought home. Each Lent, and each Month of Mary, as it comes, he wins back hundreds of these wandering sheep, and then marriages are blessed by the Church, children rescued from the shadow of parental dishonour, peace restored to divided households, embittered hearts reconciled, the dying consoled, good books distributed, the despairing restored to hope, and restitution made for ill-gotten goods. In one year alone Father Milleriot was the channel of restitutions to the amount of more than two thousand francs."

Self-devotion is an argument which few can resist. Certainly the true Frenchman cannot, and one of the causes of Father Milleriot's immense influence was his complete self-sacrifice, combined with great tact and a wonderful power of sympathy.

This influence was felt by the roughest and also the most hardened natures. A workman said to one of his comrades, "If you don't mean to turn over a new leaf, don't go to hear him. He talks to you in such a way, that you're soon caught; there's no help for it; you can't stand it."

He produced the same effect upon cultivated minds. A literary man, whom he had converted, said of him, "This orator has immense power. As for others, we all know how, in literature, the strings are pulled, but with him it is entirely different. There is about him something always fresh and unexpected, something earnest and heavenly, which seizes and overmasters, whether you will or no."

But it was more especially in what is called in France the *glose*, or few familiar words spoken before his sermons, and in which he *talked* to the congregation, about no matter what, that he was most interesting to his hearers.

The following account of one of these little prefatory conversations, (if the word may be permitted,) was given by a woman whom Father Milleriot had brought back to her religious duties after many years of neglect. While making every allowance for local colouring, we do not doubt the faithfulness of the description.

"And so," said a lady to the woman in

question, (a concierge,) "I hear you are converted. And who, then, converted you?"

"Father Milleriot, madame; a man who has not his like in all France. *Il m' a tout emberlificoté l'âme!* He quite overcame me, so that I could hold out no longer; I had to make my confession; there was no help for it. But I was so happy that, when I got home, I said to my man: 'You may think what you please; I put myself in *the box* of Father Milleriot, and confessed. He knew everything I had done, he told me all my life, and I had only to answer Yes. But I was so glad, so eased in my mind, that it was just as if the hill of Montmartre had been lifted off me.'

"No, madame, there are not two Father Milleriots in France. This father is so kind, and loves all the poor sort of people so much, that it makes him think of everything. On the eve of the First Communion he made us such a fine address; he said just like this: 'My friends,' he said, 'to-morrow will be a very great day. We shall have the happiness of receiving the good God. Now, you know, we must all be neat and clean, all in our best. And so,' he said, 'we are all going to wash our hands and faces well, and this evening the women will iron their caps and gowns, and the men will black their shoes; with a *sou's* worth of blacking you can do a good many; or if you can't manage a *sou* for blacking, try a little grease; it won't be quite so well, but it will do no harm. And while you do that,' he said, 'I will sew up a hole in the elbow of my cassock; then to-morrow I shall put on a clean white surplice, and we shall all be beautiful.'

"This little talk was after the instruction in the crypt of St. Sulpice. As the father was leaving, he turned to say, 'Now, you won't forget about the soap and the blacking; only, don't let there be any mistake, you know. It would not do to put the blacking on your faces, and the soap on your shoes!'"

The devoted charity of Father Milleriot stimulated the charity of others; thus almost all his alms were drawn from the small *bourgeoisie*, who gave freely whenever he asked them, proving that this class, so often and only too justly accused of selfishness and materialism, is, equally with other classes, ready to be generous when a generous and sympathetic guide shows it the way.

We have already mentioned the influence of

Father Milleriot even over the most hardened natures. Having given a retreat in one of the prisons, he returned a few days later to visit his beloved *detenus*. No sooner did he appear in the courtyard than all these men eagerly surrounded him, those in irons making all the haste they could to secure their share of his kindly affection, while he gave to each in turn a cordial embrace.

It was his habit, in visiting the prisons, to address himself always, in the first place, to the most hardened and obstinate. Going at once to the groups of the most hostile and ill-disposed, he would talk to them cheerfully and courteously, or playfully tap the cheek of some morose malefactor who refused to look him in the face.

Sometimes one would say to him, "Don't you remember that it was I who gave you a lot of abuse the other day?"

"Abuse? Oh yes, I remember very well; but what of that? Am I afraid of abuse? On the contrary, when I get plenty I rather enjoy it, and love you all the more in return; besides, I know quite well that you are in reality better than your words."

And when he was gone, "*Tiens!*" they

would say, " every priest is not like this one! I don't promise that I would not confess to *him.*" And almost always the words were acted on.

The next is an instance of another of Father Milleriot's thousand devices for converting sinners. Word was brought him that a man was dying. This man, not married, even at the *mairie,* was tended by his companion in guilt. Since he fell ill he had already driven away two priests, and threatened to knock down the next who dared to show himself.

This, we need not say, was a most attractive case to Father Milleriot. He went at once to the sick man's house and into his room.

At the sight of a cassock the man raised himself as much as his strength allowed, seized a stick which lay within his reach, and in a voice of fury ordered the priest out, and that instantly, unless he wanted a thrashing.

"*Mon pauvre monsieur,*" said Father Milleriot, going straight up to him, with a smile full of kindness and sympathy, "you are suffering very much, I see. This cruel fever is devouring you. Perhaps it might relieve you to give me a few strokes with your stick; if so, if it does you the least good, don't be afraid, hit as hard as you like. A few blows, more or less, make no difference; one does not die of that."

So saying, he turned and presented his shoulders, stooping so as to be exactly within range of the sword-arm. The man dropped the stick in sheer astonishment; but more than that, he was so touched and softened, that, soon afterwards, he made a good confession. Meanwhile, Father Milleriot spoke to the woman, and obtained from her, on her knees, a solemn promise of reformed life, a promise in which the sick man joined. He died, not long afterwards, in the grace of God.

There are deeds which speak more to the heart than the most eloquent sermons; a remark which applies more strongly to the next incident we have to relate, than even to the foregoing.

In a household of free-thinkers, nearly all of whom boasted that they were atheists, a poor woman lay dying. The repeated efforts of Christian persons, who were interested in her, to obtain admittance for a priest, proved unavailing, until, as in many another extreme case, Father Milleriot was applied to, in the hope that he would find or invent some means for effecting an entrance, although every one else had failed.

He did not wait for leave, but went at once to the house. When the door was opened in answer to his knock, he entered, but was insultingly refused admittance. He insisted, however, and was about to mount to the sick room, when the men, who barred his passage, threw him down upon the narrow staircase, and kicked him repeatedly with great violence. When they left off, he rose as well as he could, and stood considering a moment, and, (as he said,) rubbing his bruised sides. His assailants stood above him, and, with doubled fists and menacing gestures, uttered all the blasphemies and insults they could think of. The Father, strong in his reliance on God, and bent on the salvation of a soul, looked calmly at them, and began again to ascend the stairs, saying, with a smile, "My friends, I deserve this, but don't let us lose time,—there is a poor soul wanting to be saved!"

The threatening voices ceased, the raised arms fell, and the men, like cowed wild beasts, moved aside for the servant of God to pass. He entered the room of the dying woman, where he remained unmolested, heard her confession, and tranquilly prepared her to receive the last Sacraments of the Church.

Still more than this, he took advantage of the occasion to bring about the conversion of several members of this family, who, until that time, had been notorious for their impiety.

CHAPTER IX.

Devotion to our Blessed Lady.

GOD had bestowed upon Father Milleriot great natural gifts; but these would have been fruitless in their results with regard to souls, had they not been fertilized by the grace which is won from Him by prayer. No one more fully realized this truth than Father Milleriot himself, who, following the counsel of St. Paul, prayed "without ceasing."

Every New Year's Day, when he found himself in the midst of his people, in the crypt of St. Sulpice, to receive their greetings and good wishes, and offer them his own, he would, contrary to his custom, appear there with his hat on. Then, mounting the desk from which he often addressed them, he would take it off, saluting them all with a respectful bow; after which ceremony he would say:—

"My good friends, I have just made you all a very low bow. You must please to let that serve you until next New Year's Day. If I meet you in the street, I shall not salute you; but you must not be surprised at that. In the street I never look at any one,—I pray to the good God. In this way, as I go from St. Sulpice to the rue de Sèvres, or from my cell to the church, I manage to get time to say a good many *Paters* and *Aves*."

He was in the habit of addressing himself in particular to our Blessed Lady, to obtain the conversion of his beloved sinners. By means of the Holy Scapular of Mount Carmel and the miraculous medal, he exercised, as it were, a gentle compulsion on the Maternal Heart of Mary, who had herself attached so many favours to their faithful use, —one of the greatest being the assurance of her powerful intercession.

"How many wonderful things I could relate!" he says, in his *Souvenirs*. "Do I not owe my own life to my scapular? One day, at the Croix Rouge, I was thrown down by a waggon, and on the point of being crushed, but in the very moment of making an Act of Contrition, I was on my feet, and hurried away, declining the aid of the persons who had run to assist me."

To excite confidence in our Blessed Lady, Father Milleriot was fond of relating the story of his "Drowned Man."

"This man, having committed some dishonourable action, gave himself up to despair. As he confided in me, I kept him straight for a time, by the frequentation of the Sacraments; but, one day, all my efforts went for nothing,—he told me I should never see him again.

"'At least, grant me one favour,' I said,— 'I will give you the scapular, and you must promise me that you will never lay it aside.'

"'Father, you have been so kind to me. Yes, I promise.'

"He went away; but I said to myself *in petto*, 'My friend, I have you safe.'

"Next day his aunt came running to me. 'Father, your man is dying. Yesterday he threw himself into the Seine. He was taken out twice. He cannot swim, and yet he could not drown himself. However, he has caught a famous pleurisy, so come at once.'

"I hastened to him, and found he had kept his scapular. I heard his confession, and gave him the sacraments. A few days after he came to me with a beaming face. He was from that time a changed man."

Again. "A young needlewoman, guilty of a serious fault, shut herself up in her room, and stifled herself with the fumes of charcoal. The physician who was called in declared her to be dead. But after he had left he was beset by the thought, 'Who knows whether this poor child may have some spark of life left?' He went back, applied red-hot iron, and she awoke from her lethargy.

"Can you wonder at it?" said the good father: "she wore the scapular of our Lady; and once more was verified her solemn promise, '*In hoc moriens, æternum non patietur incendium,*'—'Whoso shall die in this, shall not suffer eternal fire.' Not long afterwards, Josephine came to confession, previous to her marriage. I say *Josephine*, because she has allowed me to mention this name in relating her wonderful preservation."

Knowing also the virtue of the miraculous medal of our Lady, and repeated instances of its effect, Father Milleriot, who gave it to everybody he could, was rewarded for his boundless confidence in the assistance vouchsafed by the Blessed Virgin to those who wore it, by the singular favours he obtained in cases apparently hopeless.

He has told us the story of the man whom he called *mon noyé*. He tells also of another called *mon pendu*. A worthy and honest man, whom the father knew, was the victim of a false accusation, which completely took away his character. In his distress of mind he hung himself, and only escaped death by the almost miraculous protection of God. Father Milleriot, who had given him the miraculous medal, was informed of what had happened, and hastened to see the man.

"Well, my friend, and how did you manage not to kill yourself?"

"Don't speak of it. I cannot make it out. I know that I had made sure of a good strong rope, and that I threw myself off into space."

" I took advantage of the occasion to obtain from him a regular confession, and from that time he has been a good, practical Christian, which he was not before."

On this theme Father Milleriot was inexhaustible. "Listen," he would say, "to some more remarkable instances of the intervention of Divine Providence on behalf of those who wear the miraculous medal.

"Six soldiers came to the meeting of our working-men before leaving for the Crimea, and I gave them each a medal. While away, they took part in the hottest engagements of this terrible campaign, and saw multitudes of their comrades fall around them. All six came home without a wound."

"A child of four years old fell from the fourth storey of a house on to the pavement. In two hours afterwards he was playing about the street. I went myself to verify the fact. He had two days before received the miraculous medal. His mother, full of gratitude to the Blessed Virgin, from a Protestant became a Catholic."

"A man, distinguished by his birth and learning, was dying, at an advanced age. When the curé of the parish had visited him, '*Monsieur le curé*,' said the sick man, 'I thank you for your zeal; but I am without faith; I am a Voltairian.' And the good priest withdrew in tears. However, he attempted a second visit.

"'Monsieur le curé, I beg of you not to come any more.'

"I was applied to by the sick man's family. 'Father, if only you would go to him.'

"'I, when this holy man has failed? Impossible. But if you will help me I will send the dying man a person who will not fail.'

"'Whom?'

"'The Blessed Virgin.'

"'How?'

"'Take this miraculous medal to M. de —— and simply ask him to unite his intention to the prayers that will be made for him.'

"'He never will.'

"'Christian family! if, all together, you do not induce him to wear this medal, I shall say you have no tact, no *esprit*.'

"Unwilling not to have *esprit*, they contrived to obtain the acceptance of the precious medal. It was only what I had expected. Then, as I had been schoolfellow to a relation of the family, the sick man did not refuse to receive me as a friend. Still, the ladies were full of anxiety. 'Father,' they said, 'how shall you manage?'

"'How? the thing is half done. Take me to him, and you will soon see that which will rejoice your hearts.'

"I was taken to the sick man, and began

by thanking him for the honour he did me in allowing me to see him. Then I spoke with pleasure of his generosity and beneficence to the poor, for these were well known to me. By degrees I was left alone with him, and, feeling myself supported by our Blessed Lady, I asked him a few questions, which he answered with the simplicity of a child. At last, pushing my point, I obtained from him a confession, fully sufficient, considering his state. Then I sent for his family to come in.

"'Well, my dear sir, say to those present if you are content.'

"'I am, very.'

"'Have we made together a good little confession?'

"'Certainly.'

"'Do you not feel happy in the thought that God has granted you forgiveness?'

"'Indeed I do.'

"'Well, then, my venerable friend, and now you will receive the great Physician of the world, our Lord Himself.'

"'Most willingly.'

"'And you will have a privilege which neither these ladies nor I possess, you will make your communion without fasting; and in order to do this, you will receive the Holy Oils for your body as well as the Holy Eucharist for your soul.'

"'Let all be as you think well.'

"And all was done while the dying man was in full possession of his consciousness. Next day when I visited him he was unconscious, but I thought he would know me...... I went to his bedside, and said, 'Monsieur de ——, do you know who I am?'

"'*Parbleu!* I should think I do!'

"I then suggested the thoughts which should fill the mind of a Christian during his last moments in this world, and before leaving gave him the plenary absolution, *in articulo mortis*. The next day he was dead."

Another account, given in the *Souvenirs*, of an officer of eighty-two, is very similar to the foregoing, except that the aged colonel, after being by the same means brought back to religion after seventy years of neglect, recovered his health also, and, after many months, fell asleep, full of faith, peacefully in the Lord.

CHAPTER X.

Devotion to Holy Church, and the Pope.

THIS faithful servant of Mary, strong in that filial confidence so often visibly rewarded, could not take in the idea that his heavenly Mother could refuse him anything. When some matter, about which he had prayed to her very earnestly, did not turn out as he had desired, the good Father permitted himself humbly to remonstrate with her, and pleaded and complained with that familiarity with which the saints plead and complain to God Himself. In excuse for this, and lest it should seem like irreverence, he would say to his dear people, to whom he freely opened his heart, "My friends, now hear what I have to say. For many long years before the authoritative definition of the Immaculate Conception, I offered to God all my free* Masses for obtaining the solemn

---

* i.e. The Masses not promised to be said for any particular intention.

promulgation of this dogma of the faith. I used to say to the holy Virgin: 'My blessed Mother, I am 'altogether worthless, but our Lord, whom I have so often offered upon the altar for your intention, ah, is not *That* a worthy offering?' And so, when the decree was given, I could without too much temerity congratulate myself on having done something to contribute towards it, and I rejoiced together with you. Immediately after this definition, I began next to offer all my free Masses for the triumph of holy Church, and for the intentions of the infallible successor of St. Peter.

"Well, the Ecumenical Council also defined this great privilege of the Vicar of Jesus Christ. 'It was you, holy Virgin, who obtained this from the divine goodness, and it was a great thing. But let me speak yet a word. Since I have, from that time until now, continued to offer up so many Masses for the deliverance of the august captive who is under your protection, why is it, holy Mother, that you suffer him to remain in imprisonment so long? May I not whisper in your ear a murmur, that so it should be?' There, my friends, now you have my excuse......"

Father Milleriot inspired all under his direction with his own devotion towards the holy Church and her earthly Head. His people, touched by the Holy Father's misfortunes, imposed on themselves sacrifices which, however small in themselves they may appear, were often almost heroic. Among other instances we find, in his *Souvenirs*, the following:

"An old man of eighty-three came to me one day at St. Sulpice. His garb bespoke more than poverty,—utter indigence. 'My father,' he said, 'here are three francs for the Peter's Pence.'

"'God will reward your good deed, my friend, and all the more because you do not seem to be a millionaire.'

"'True; I am not rich, but I have a heart. I love Pius IX., and I made these little savings out of my mouth.'

"'That was noble of you! But is it not too great a privation? Suppose you give half this sum to the Pope, and keep the other half, so as not to eat your bread too dry?'

"'No; all for the Pope.'

"I had to accept it. 'But,' I said, 'I have an idea. A soul so generous must have its place marked in heaven. You have the religion of the heart, and it is the best; but is there something which may still be wanting to you? Tell me, good father, are we a little behindhand with our religious duties?'

"'Oh, no doubt as to that; but they will come later.'

"'Why later? Who knows what may happen? Why not to-day?'

"'I did not come here to confess.'

"'I am aware of that; but to a man like you it is an easy matter.'

"'Father, I am not prepared.'

"'That may be, but I am quite prepared to hear you. Now, let me only ask you a few questions; answer Yes or No. You will soon feel very glad.'

"As he was silent, I saw that I might go on. I asked the customary questions, to which he answered with great simplicity. The confession was made. It only remained to complete it sacramentally, and to arouse in this simple soul the necessary contrition. The good old man entered of his own accord into the sentiments suggested to him, and submitted to everything with the docility of a child; and then how great was his joy!

"'Ah, my good father,' he exclaimed, 'how

happy I am! What a good confession! what a grace to have had absolution! Yes, it is the happiest day of my life.'

"And he went away, his face bathed in tears, leaving me rejoicing in his joy."

This worthy man had brought the offering of the poor, and Father Milleriot, fulfilling the promise of God in the Gospel, had given him a hundredfold in return. Never did he neglect an opportunity to instruct, reconcile, and convert. When souls did not seek *him*, he, like the Good Shepherd, hastened to seek *them*, and rested not until they were found.

One day a woman hurried to the confessional of Father Milleriot. "Father, come quickly," she said, "a man is dying, not far from here; he is a *sergent de ville*, and he consents to see you."

The Father left the confessional at once, saying to the people who were awaiting their turn, "A little moment of patience; I shall be back soon; meanwhile pray, all of you, for the salvation of a dying man." We continue from his own account.

"I crossed the Place St. Sulpice, threaded the rue du Vieux Colombier, hurrying as fast as I could without venturing to run, as I remembered the rule which says, 'Let not your walk be very rapid without great necessity, and even then decorum must be observed.' In the midst of these thoughts, I met a detachment of firemen running with their engine to extinguish a fire broken out in the neighbourhood, and, at this sight, said to myself, 'What! here are men running to put out a material fire, and am I not to run to extinguish the fire for souls? Run, *fireman of souls!* run to snatch from eternal flames a soul redeemed by the Blood of Jesus!' I ran, therefore, though careful to run with decorum, and arrived by the side of the dying man only a few minutes before death. The confession did not take long. I had only the time strictly necessary to allow of his receiving the last sacraments from the hands of the guardian priest. Then I hastened back to my confessional, and thanked my penitents for the succour of their prayers."

CHAPTER XI.

The Society of St. Francis Xavier, and the "Holy Family."

THROUGHOUT the long years of his ministry, Father Milleriot was the life and soul of two admirable associations, the Society of St. Francis Xavier, and the "Holy Family" of St. Sulpice.

The Society of St. Francis Xavier, a work for the mutual assistance of working-men, was founded by the venerable M. Hamon, Curé of St. Sulpice. Its spiritual director was Father Milleriot, and its president M. Gaillardin. Its meetings took place once a month, at 36, rue de l'Ouest, to which was attached its chapel of *Notre Dame des Bonnes Ouvres*. From seven hundred to eight hundred men never failed to be present at these reunions, in which, after the religious exercises, the interest of the members was sustained by a varied succession of addresses and instructions, chiefly on topics of religion, morality, or relating to questions of the day more or less in connection with religion. These were intermingled with songs, instrumental music, and other harmless kinds of entertainment. The excellent behaviour of these men, the attention with which they listened to the familiar allocutions addressed to them, the mutual understanding at once established between the speaker and the audience, each so well suited to the other,—all this proved that the Parisian working classes are not so averse to religion as is commonly supposed. The important matter is to know how first to win their confidence, to bring out and make use of their good points, to revive their religious faith, too often dormant and smothered for a lapse of many years; and in all this, Father Milleriot was perfectly at home.

M. Louis Veuillot relates an incident which shows the natural generosity of these men of the people, and their readiness to make sacrifices for the good of others still poorer than themselves.

The president, after giving an account of the state of the work, its general fund, &c., proposed to levy upon this fund of savings the sum of one hundred francs for the benefit of the suffering weavers in the Departments, at a time when there was great scarcity of work. The proposal was received with unanimous acclamation, amidst which were cries of "Not enough! not enough!"* With difficulty Father Milleriot made himself heard. "My friends," he said, "I highly applaud your kind feelings and generous hearts, but we must in prudence consider the interests of your exchequer." His powerful voice was overpowered by the proposal to "Double the sum." And this proposal being put to the vote, was received with a salvo of applause. It was further suggested that the customary evening's collection should on that occasion be appropriated to the same purpose. Then and there this collection was made in the meeting, and found to reach the amount of another hundred francs. Great was the general joy; so much so, that some gentlemen present, touched by the generous enthusiasm of these poor men, asked why facts like these should not be published, facts so honourable alike to the French character, and above all to religion. "And this," adds the editor of the *Univers*, "we

* L'Univers, 1 Fév., 1862.

ourselves witnessed, and we would make it known to all who have a mind to understand and a heart to feel."

It was in this Society of St. François Xavier that Pierre Olivaint, while a professor at the university, made his first trial of arms; and, when named Superior of the Jesuit Fathers in the rue de Sèvres, he watched with the greatest sympathy and interest the good progress of the work, in the able hands of Father Milleriot.

With regard to his other favourite work, we give his own words:

"The *Sainte Famille* is an association of Christian people of small means,—men and women,—small shopkeepers, needlewomen, servants, and others. From the time of its foundation it has numbered among its members so many returns to a life of practical religion, so many holy and good deaths, that in it the words of our Blessed Lord have indeed been verified, 'Blessed are the poor, for theirs is the kingdom of heaven.'

"Of these two works I could say to the Abbé Hamon, when made Curé of St. Sulpice, that they were the two fairest gems in his crown.

"And yet, in this model parish, thanks to this holy priest and to his excellent vicaires, good is done in an ever-increasing proportion. Every class and every form of need is, so to speak, taken possession of by Christian charity in its fullest sense. The aged, who have nothing to live upon, by the Little Sisters of the Poor; apprentices by the "Patronages" (of St. Joseph, for instance); men of the world, by the Confraternity of the Blessed Sacrament; there are evening schools for working-men, orphanages for girls, associations and their periodical reunions for youths and young men; Sisters of St. Vincent de Paul for the sick poor; *crêches* for infants, &c., &c.; so that the maternal care of the Church penetrates everywhere, and leaves nothing forgotten, while all these works complete and sustain one another, their action utilized and directed by the venerated pastor whose greatest influence is exercised by his own saintly and laborious life.

"But to return to the *Sainte Famille*. It numbered about two thousand members, consequently the number of confessions in this association amounted to about twenty thousand a year, the one being consequent on the other."

The annual retreat for the *Sainte Famille* was given by Father Milleriot in the crypt of St. Sulpice during the week preceding the Feast of the Assumption. Before the instruction began, he seemed to be everywhere at once, arranging for the accommodation of the numerous *retraitants,* mounting the pulpit to give directions, going round the aisles to unearth from their obscurity and out-of-the-way corners men who were afraid or shy of showing themselves. These he would take familiarly by the arm; sometimes he would even embrace them, and then lead them gently into the nave, where there were the best places.

Sometimes in his addresses to his dear people, he would seem to be carried away by a sort of impassioned enthusiasm, but he never allowed it to carry him too far. The excellent president of the work, M. de la Villeboisnet, sometimes showed a little anxiety on these occasions as to what the good Father might be going to say, but Father Milleriot, with his kindly smile, would bend towards him, and say in a low voice, "Don't be uneasy, my dear friend; even when I run away I know where I must stop."

"Almost all the two thousand members of the *Sainte Famille*," wrote Father Milleriot to the Very Rev. Father General,* in 1867, "are persons who have been brought back to religion after a neglect of many years. The Very Rev. Father Roothan† was so good as to say to me on this subject, 'Do not be jealous of any one in the Company; you have your share, and a large one.' You, reverend father, know me through and through; you know how much and how little I am worth. I am no preacher in the ordinary sense of the word. The Stations of Lent and Advent are not in my line so much as the evening meetings,—the people, the masses. So far my strength keeps up well, and, in the ordinary course of things, I can work thus for some years to come."

When he wrote these lines, Father Milleriot was nearly sixty-six years old. Instead of thinking of rest, he said, with St. Martin, "*Non recuso laborem*," and it was not until fifteen years afterwards that he was compelled

---

* The Very Rev. Father Beckx.
† Predecessor of Father Beckx.

by complete exhaustion to resign the charge of these two associations so dear to his heart. On the 16th of March, 1880, he thus wrote to the Curé of St. Sulpice:

"*Monsieur le Curé,*—For thirty-six years I have had charge of the *Sainte Famille*. My strength is no longer sufficient for it, and I am therefore obliged to give it up. The same reasons of health and of my great age,—over eighty years,—compel me to lay aside also the direction of the Society of St. Francis Xavier, after thirty-two years of unremitting care. You will easily replace me, *monsieur le curé*, by one of your *vicaires*. For myself, I shall still have the ministry of the confessional, which I hope to resume very soon. May I thus devote the remainder of my days in preparing to appear before God.

"Your poor old servant in Jesus Christ,

"MILLERIOT, S.J."

CHAPTER XII.

Mingled Strength and Gentleness of Character.—The Commune.

THOSE who have read these pages thus far, will have formed by this time a fairly exact idea of the character of the man, and the virtue of the religious. A few more touches may still be given to a portrait which gains in interest the more closely it can be made to resemble the original.

In one of his addresses to the *Sainte Famille*, Father Milleriot had commented on the saying of St. Francis de Sales, when told of a pious man whose only drawback was his melancholy air. "Ah," said the bishop, "if he is a saint who is melancholy, he is a melancholy saint." The audience fully comprehended the lesson conveyed by the words, namely, that we must serve God joyously. The preacher himself set the example.

One of his hearers in particular showed hi

that she did not forget it. This worthy woman, a seller of needles and thread, was wheeling her little store of merchandize along the rue du Bac, and singing her accustomed song, "*Achetez du fil : achetez des aiguilles !*" when she caught sight of the Father on the other side of the street, and continued her song with a variation suited to the occasion: "*Achetez du fil, achetez des aiguilles ! Un saint triste est un triste saint. C'est le Père Milleriot qui l'a dit.*"

> "Buy my needles, buy my thread,
> He's a sad saint, the saint who is sad;
> This is what Father Milleriot said."

The passers-by laughed, and the Father, being a "joyous saint," laughed also.

One day, having been delayed, he was hurrying into the confessional, and struck his head violently against the door. "Let me alone; it is nothing at all!" he said to the penitents, who crowded round him; "you see, I like to give myself the bump of confession." He added afterwards, in speaking of the incident, and in apology for the somewhat vulgar expression he had used, "I am a Burgundian, it is true, but I am equal to a Breton; blows on the head are not dangerous to *me*."

If, however, he saw others suffer, it was quite another matter. His heart was full of sympathy and compassion. In his *Souvenirs* we find the following:

"On my way from St. Sulpice, I was one day returning by the *Chemin des Ecoliers*, when I met a little lad of about twelve, carrying an enormous mirror, which must have weighed at least thirty kilogrammes (sixty pounds). The poor child was bathed in perspiration, and ready to fall from fatigue.

"'My little friend, how far have you to carry that glass?'

"'To the other side of Paris.'

"'Impossible! you will fall under such a load.'

"'No help for it. If I don't, my *patron* will dismiss me, and my mother will beat me. Already I have got a bad hurt inside from carrying heavy goods; but all the same, I must get on as best I can.'

"Full of pity for the poor little fellow, I engaged a porter for a certain sum to carry the glass. However, I had the utmost difficulty to persuade the boy to accept my proposal. I managed it at last by slipping into his hand a two-franc piece for his own, and then I watched him following the porter with light step and beaming face. I hope this child will remember that a priest has been kind to him, and this may one day bring him happiness."

Thus the supernatural thought of God and of souls was ever present with him, even in acts which seem prompted only by the spontaneous impulse of the heart. He was fond of quoting some words he had heard from Mgr. de Quélen, that "there are men who need but the touch of a finger to be led to the practice of religion." Whenever an opportunity offered, he never failed to give the "touch of the finger," in the hope that God would do the rest.

The dreadful period of the commune, far from lessening his courage, kindled in the heart of Father Milleriot a truly warlike ardour. There was much of the soldier in this priest.

By order of the insurrectional power, the Church of St. Sulpice was closed and guarded, the *fëdérès* pretending that the *Versaillais* had spies or agents hidden in the vaults.

Father Milleriot saw, however, no reason for altering his usual habits. He presented himself boldly before the closed doors, and after some ineffectual endeavours to open them, came upon a group of sinister-faced men, forming a sort of outpost near the rue Servandoni. He attempted to parley, but they repulsed and threatened him.

"Who are you?" they asked.

"The Father of the working-men. I beg from the rich to give to the poor. Besides, I am no *capon; I disguise myself as a priest,* as you see, to assist deserving people."

"Be off with you, or else......"

"Come, come, my friends, have you a mind to shoot me? What would be the use? An old individual like me, of nearly seventy-two years of age? Why, my skin would not be fit even to cover a drum." So saying, he bowed courteously, and marched away.

The fédérés applauded, and their captain could not help saying, "All the same, that's a brave man, let him pass."

Father Milleriot thus relates another of his little adventures at the same time:

"It was the 24th of May. Six weeks after I had been forced away from my community, and obliged to seek a refuge among friends, I found myself in an awkward predicament. Absent momentarily from my abode, it was necessary to return thither. As I passed along the rue de Sèvres, bullets whistled in all directions, so I hastened into the first court of which I found the door ajar, and there waited until I could leave it with less danger. When a moment's respite allowed of this, I went into the rue du Cherche-Midi, reached the corps de garde in front of the military prison, and addressed myself to a corporal of the fédérés. 'Friend,' I said, 'give me two of your men for an escort. I have to see the dying wife of one of my artisans. She asks for me that I may console her husband a little.'

"'Well,' said the corporal, after a certain hesitation, 'well, citizen, I will accompany you myself with one of my men.'

"And we set out. Behind me, a poor woman, in tears, seemed to claim my protection. 'My husband is ill,' she said; 'let me pass also, that I may go to him.'

"'Follow me, *ma petite*,' I said, 'we will both pass, never fear. Is there some danger?' I added, addressing my man.

"'Come along, all the same; when necessary, we will give you warning, and you must stoop your backs down.'

"We advanced, and reached the Place St. Sulpice. At a given signal we lowered our backs, and before long I entered my abode safe and sound, made my escort drink to my health, and after giving them a merited gratification, we parted, the best friends in the world.

"But some of my poor people had seen me passing through the streets between two of the national guard. 'Alas!' they said one to another, 'they are taking our poor Father Milleriot also to prison!' when, on the contrary, it was I who was taking *them*. But the alarm was abroad. A few days afterwards I was peaceably seated in my confessional, reciting my breviary, when a woman approached, and in a bewildered state of mind addressed me in these incredible words:

"'Father, is it true that you have been shot?'

"'Alas, yes,' I answered, smiling; 'only be sure you say nothing about it to anybody.'"

One day, still during the commune, Father Milleriot was going his customary rounds among the sick, and marched on, his hands thrust into his wide sleeves, and murmuring prayers, when he met a gentleman, very correctly dressed, of lofty stature and distinguished appearance, who saluted him in passing.

The Father stopped, took off his hat, went straight up to the gentleman, and taking hold of his hand lest he should escape, said to him then and there, "Pardon, my good sir, *(mon digne monsieur,)* have we made our Easter Communion this year?"

"*Oui, mon père.*"

"Ah, that is all right then; that is well; let us so continue." And Father Milleriot, satisfied as to the condition of this good Christian, pursued his way as before.

The "*digne monsieur*" was no other than the Abbé d'Hulst, since then Vicar-General of Paris, and rector of the Catholic university, and who, in order to be able to fulfil the duties of his ministry, had found it necessary to put on the dress of a layman. The story was told to the Superior of the rue de Sèvres, who acquainted Father Milleriot with his blunder.

"So much the worse for me," he answered, "if I have made a simpleton of myself; but I freely own that I feel no contrition for it in the least."

When at last the French army entered Paris, nothing could keep Father Milleriot in his room in the rue d'Assas. There were so many wounded and dying to tend, console, or absolve. He had just left his abode, and was hurrying towards the Luxembourg, when the gunpowder, stored there from the commencement of the siege, exploded, producing frightful destruction. All the windows in the neighbourhood were shattered, many persons killed, and many more thrown down and more or less injured. Father Milleriot escaped with nothing worse than a shower of broken glass upon his hat. When he returned to his room, great was his thankfulness to have quitted it in time. Everything in it was shivered to fragments by the explosion, and had he remained there a few moments longer, he must have been either killed or seriously hurt. He records this escape, together with other favours of Divine Providence towards him, in order to excite in others his own confidence in God.

CHAPTER XIII.

The Proscript.—Last Days.

THE execution of the tyrannical decrees of March 29th, 1880, struck Father Milleriot a blow from which he never recovered. His courage and faith never failed for a moment; but his heart was stricken, and his end hastened by the injustice of men. The odious work of the commune being continued, ten years later, by those in power, with the same violence, but a violence made still more odious by being joined with lying and hypocrisy, Father Milleriot was driven from his holy home in the rue de Sèvres, and from the cell which, for so many laborious years, had been, as it were, the shrine of so many long communings with God, of mortification, and of prayer.

On the 30th of June, 1880, by four o'clock in the morning, the executioners of the March decrees were at their evil work. The residence in the rue de Sèvres was invaded, and its doors broken open, in spite of the indignant protest of a large number of senators, deputies, and other honourable personages, who had gone thither to uphold, not only the rights of conscience, but also to defend the civil rights and liberties thus shamelessly violated by the loudest professors of " liberty, equality, and fraternity."

Cell after cell was broken open, and its venerable occupant forced out into the street. Each time that a Father appeared on the threshold, leaning on the arm of one of the Christian gentlemen who had gone to the residence as a defender or a *witness*, the street resounded anew with shouts of " *Vive les Jésuites ! Vive la liberté !*"

The sergents de ville, in perplexity, did not know how to act, having the mob of ruffians *with* them, and honest men *against* them. The two *commissaires de police*, pale and embarrassed, stuttered and hesitated like the very individuals whom they are in the habit of collaring, being, like them, engaged in the very act of housebreaking, or, as they would hear it called in court, "*en flagrant délit d'escalade et d'effraction.*" Their prefect, M.

Andrieux, who has recently attempted to excuse himself to his electors for the criminal act which he then presided over and enforced, put on a threatening attitude, which alarmed nobody.*

The operation was a long one, from the time occupied in breaking open each separate cell, and also by the passive resistance of its rightful occupant, more than one aged Father having to be literally carried out by the housebreakers.

About seven o'clock, Father Milleriot, his hat on, and an umbrella under his arm, suddenly appeared in the interior court, which was crowded by the agents of the police. His air was severe, his glance flashed more sternly than was its wont, his words were brief and determined.

"I see him, I hear him yet," writes Father Clair. "One felt that it cost him a strong effort to contain the indignation ready to burst forth."

"Make way," he said, "I am half-an-hour late for St. Sulpice."

The poor sergents de ville respectfully made

---

* See the address of M. Andrieux, préfêt de police, to his electors at Arbresle.

way, and when Father Clair said to them, "*That is Father Milleriot,*" the interest with which they gazed after him until he was lost sight of in the street, showed plainly that, to many among them, this was a well-known name.

Driven from his poor cell, Father Milleriot found a refuge in the rue de la Chaise, where, from his window, he could see his beloved house, closed and deserted. Nothing, however, in his rule of life was changed. He continued to rise at three o'clock daily, and sometimes even earlier still. As he carefully renewed this permission every month, his Superior one day asked him why he should do this, as it was too fatiguing for him.

"If I did not," he answered, "I could not have my *two hours'* meditation before my five o'clock Mass; it is necessary."

"At least, then, modify your diet. I am not satisfied about your breakfast,—a little coffee, without milk or bread, and taken standing; nor your supper,—a little soup and vegetables or cheese. Why, this is how I *fast*, for my part."

"But not I, father. I am dispensed from fasting on account of my great age, but I have lived thus for the last twenty years, and if you will allow me I will live so to the end."

Only a few months before his death, Father Milleriot, already much enfeebled by illness, went to see one of his former pupils, about some charitable work in which both were interested. His weakness was so great, that, contrary to his custom, he had been obliged to take a cab. He arrived, pale and exhausted, breathing with difficulty, but not uttering a word of complaint. The conversation ended, the master and mistress of the house, alarmed at his state of prostration, entreated him to take a little wine, but he said, with a tone peculiar to himself, "My children, for more than fifty years Father Milleriot has not been thirsty between his meals." And he left without taking anything.

From the day of his expulsion, his strength rapidly declined. If any one asked him about his health, he always said, "Don't let us talk about myself; it is a waste of time."

If allusion were made to the painful events of the 30th of June, he would say quickly, "Do not speak of *that*." Once, however, when a young man, in the flush of his indignation, declared his inability to mention certain names, and at the same time contain his anger, he answered, "Oh, I can understand that. You are not the only one......But," he immediately added, "Let us pray for them, that at least one in a thousand of them may be converted. It is so difficult, after what they have done, and with what they are doing still."

On returning from St. Sulpice in the evening, he went his usual way by the Croix Rouge, and then, instead of turning to the right for the rue de la Chaise, he always kept on, up the rue de Sèvres to number thirty-five, the residence from whence the Fathers had been driven. Here he would stand for some moments before the sealed-up door of the chapel, where, from the day of its closing, the ground has, by pious hands, been daily strewn with flowers. And then, gravely and sorrowfully, the proscript Father would turn back in the direction of the little chamber which was the home of his exile.

When no longer able to walk, he took a conveyance for the short distance to St. Sulpice, and then dragged himself as best he could to his confessional. In vain his medical adviser endeavoured to dissuade him; the aged Father gaily improvised a verse in which he intended poetry to win the day against prudence.

> " Confesser est ma vie,
> Non confesser ma mort.
> Permettez, je vous prie,
> Que je ne meure encor."

" To hear confession is my life, to hear it *not*, my death ;
Permit me, then, that *yet* I need not draw my latest breath."

CHAPTER XIV.

A Holy Death.

DEATH was fast approaching. He foresaw it more plainly than he chose to say. In the *Journal de mes Ministères*, faithfully kept for forty years, there is, towards the close of 1879, a sort of general summing up, in which occur the following figures, "Confessions heard, 705,300."

In his aged handwriting, still fine and clear, but now very trembling, he wrote: "Fourth quarter of 1880; total of confessions during the year, nineteen thousand." And further on: "three sick; three hundred francs in alms."

The last thought of this year was for his beloved sick and poor.

In February, 1881, Father Milleriot was unable to leave his room, and, in a little while, his bed. His Superior remained almost constantly by the side of the venerable religious, and it is to him that we are indebted for the account of the last days of this holy life, and the holy death which crowned it. These notes, written day by day, we give exactly as they were put down at the time.

"What would happen, father, if, some fine morning, I came to say that, in another week, you would be in Paradise?"

"Reverend father, if you came to tell me such news as this, I should be so glad of it, so glad, that I should very likely die of joy instead of waiting another week, and so make you tell a story. But, for all that," he added, "when you have the good news to bring, don't fail to let me have it."

"Bonjour, mon père: what have you been doing since yesterday?"

"Doing? I have been growing in weariness as much as *that*," (and he stretched out his arms as wide as he could;) "and with weariness as much as that," he continued, "I have grown in patience as much as *this;*" and he brought the palms of his hands together, leaving no space.

"Then we have been a little impatient?"

A HOLY DEATH. 135

"Oh, not at all," he answered, cheerfully; "patience is an extract, an elixir."

"You are still, then, ready for a little jest?"

"One ought to be so, otherwise one would be insupportable to one's poor neighbour."

"It seems long since I saw you, father. Have you still been growing in weariness?"

"Not the least in the world. I have had something better than that."

"You have been suffering?"

"Yes."

"And praying?"

"Yes."

"Praying to suffer less?"

"*Par exemple!* Certainly not! What? There are sinners offending God all day long, dying, being lost for ever, and I should pray to suffer *less?* Come, come!......Poor sinners! poor sinners! I have been praying for *them.*"

"And how are you to-day?"

"How? Always suffering, and always glad......"

"You suffer much?"

"Enormously."

"You offer up this suffering for sinners?"

"Yes. How much they are to be pitied! They have in *this* life none of the consolations which we have,—the only true ones; and they run to perdition in the *next*. We ought indeed to do something for them. I do my little utmost,—I suffer and pray."

"And willingly, with all your heart?"

"Always."

"And you suffer also a little for yourself?"

"Certainly. I do not forget that there is a purgatory."

"Those who suffer much," he said, one day, "in order to suffer *well*, throw themselves into the arms of God's mercy. I am not doing this just now."

"Then what are you doing?"

"I throw myself into the arms of His justice, and this is what I say to Him: 'My God, I am suffering very much. You permit this, and You are right. I have not stolen this suffering, but earned it. Give me still more, if it be Your will; it is justice. Double it, (for You can,) and You will not exceed what I deserve; triple it, even, and I shall still be in advance.' I say all this very sincerely, and then, do you know what happens?

The good God is touched, and cannot go on. See how one finds the mercy and goodness of God everywhere, even in His justice!"

He was lying perfectly still, not asleep, but absorbed. I went near, but he took no notice. I doubted if he knew me. "Father," I said, "it is I."

"That is well; what are you come for?"

"Your bulletin of health, dear father."

"My bulletin of health," he repeated, rousing himself; "ah, that requires some reflection." He thought a moment, then in a tone of exaggerated depth and solemnity he said: "Here it is: sleep, none; weakness, great; *appétit, petit ;*" and he smiled, adding pleasantly in his natural voice, "but one would not be sad for this. A saint who is sad is a sad saint."

February 25.—All day he had been restless and full of suffering. No nourishment had been taken, and his weakness made alarming progress. Father Matignon sent for me, asking if I did not consider it prudent to think about administering the last sacraments.

I approached Father Milleriot, who, on

seeing me, became no longer restless, and at his request I heard his confession. Then I mentioned what I had come to suggest, but he thought it premature, for, although he desired to receive Extreme Unction in the full clearness of his understanding, and consciousness, and will, he was equally anxious not to lose the full benefit of the sacrament, and said that one ought not to forestall the hour marked by God. I pressed the matter, however; he listened in silence, and yielded.

"Father," he said, "what you have now been saying I have myself said very often and very easily to others, but I have not found it so easy a matter to hear it myself. Poor human nature! she is full of vitality, father, and rebels at the thought of death. To overcome her I must cling and climb. I climb, I have managed it, but not without effort. What poor creatures we are!"

Next morning, at four o'clock, he sent word to me that he was *converted*, and wished to see me. When I arrived, "I am very tired," he said, "but I am ready. There is no need for putting off what we agreed upon yesterday."

"Would you not wish some of the fathers to be present?"

"No; they are scattered in one place or another: some to make their meditation, some saying their Mass. It would be difficult to assemble them. Father Matignon is here, with two brothers, he will represent the rest. My hoarseness would not allow me to speak to them at my ease; you must be my interpreter."

"Have you something to say to them?"

"Yes, three things. First, by my negligence in the observance of the Rules,—those of silence and the others,—I have disedified them, and I beg their pardon for it. Then, by my rough and off-hand ways, or bad temper, I may have given them pain; I do not remember, but it is possible, and for this also I beg their pardon. Lastly, if they, unconsciously or otherwise, have chanced also to mortify me,—not that I know of anything in particular,—I pardon them, too, with all my heart. And now, dear and reverend father, you will give me one more good absolution, then the Holy Communion, and then Extreme Unction."

And all was done as he desired it, in the utmost piety and peace.

Before leaving, I gave him one more benediction, and he affectionately thanked me.

"You feel better, father?" I asked.

"In body, no; but in my soul, yes, much, very much better."

During the whole day he was oppressed and exhausted, and saw scarcely any one. I did not go to him until evening. When I entered, he said, "I was longing for you to come."

"Father, I thought of your fatigue, and your desire to be alone with God, and therefore delayed my visit."

"Yes, visits tire me."

"Mine shall be short."

"On the contrary, I want it to be long. I am going to fatigue myself, but I wish to fatigue myself and not others. Sit down. And first I want to thank you; I thanked you once, but I wish to thank you again."

"And why? for the trouble I gave you yesterday?"

"No, no; but for your charity towards me. Never can I thank you enough for the immense service of this morning, as well as for yesterday......Do you know, that to be of the

A HOLY DEATH. 141

same opinion as one's Superior sometimes requires an heroic effort?"

"This was the case yesterday, was it not?"

"I do not know, it is not for me to judge; I leave that to God."

"God has given you a great grace, father, while leaving you your natural repugnances, to give you strength to overcome them."

"He has indeed. I had yesterday a famous push on the shoulder towards my passage through purgatory; it was needed. The good God is always full of goodness. But I have something else to say to you; it is on the subject of my agony."

"In the matter of conscience you have nothing which troubles you?"

"No."

"Neither do you, then, let yourself be troubled about the moment when God will call you. St. Joseph will be there, and our Blessed Lady. Let us have confidence. Our Lady is so kind, St. Joseph also. You have confidence, have you not?"

"Since I have received Extreme Unction my state is this: I lie stretched out and quite still in my bed, and I say to our Lord: 'My kind Master, I am here, and here I stay waiting until death shall come to take me. If he come, it will be by Your permission, and all will be well; but in case You should not permit him, let us say no more about it; I am quite content.'"

"You still have, then, some little fear of death?"

"No, I do not fear it, neither do I desire it. The great saints desired it: that shows that I am but a little saint. I commend myself to the will of God."

"Yes, to the will of God, in peace and calm, in full and filial trust, without pre-occupation."

"I am not pre-occupied. I occupy myself about the moment of my agony. There is a detail which we will settle, if you will be so kind. It is this. I shall die choked. I shall be conscious up to the last, but I shall lose my speech a little before it. You will be here, and will see the efforts I shall make to speak, but in vain, for my lips will be paralyzed. At that moment you will speak to God for me, and I will inwardly say this: 'My God, I believe, I adore, I love, and I hope,' and I will end with the *Suscipe* of St. Ignatius. My lips will be useless to me, but you will lend me yours, to give a body to my prayer. With you here will be Father Lefebvre, Father Matignon, and the brothers. Should you, for any reason, prefer to give to Father Lefebvre the little commission to do me this last service, I thank both you and him for it beforehand."

The first of March was passed very calmly. Suffering had ceased, but the weakness was extreme, and the respiration rapid.

About a quarter past eleven at night, Father Matignon, who was watching with two brothers, sent for me. I got up, and with Father Lefebvre repaired to the rue de la Chaise. I approached the dying father, and pressed his hand. "My dear father," I said, "you know me."

For all answer he began immediately, in a strong voice, to say the *Confiteor*. At the *mea culpa* he stopped, and in a softer voice, though still aloud, he made his confession. As he was rather long about this, I observed to him that as for some time past he had confessed almost daily, he might, unless anything special were troubling him, abridge the rest, and accuse himself in general of all the faults of his life.

"Yes," he answered, "I renew my accusation of them;" and in the same tone in which he had begun it, he resumed and finished the *Confiteor.*

I imposed a prayer as his penance. "Let us say it altogether at once," he said, "before the absolution; it is the surest way."

We did so. I pronounced the absolution, and after the sacramental formula I added, "*Vade in pace.*"

"*In pace,*" he answered, and these were his last words. After some moments he attempted to speak, but could not; his lips were becoming paralyzed.

The moment that he had indicated with so much precision had arrived. Father Lefebvre drew near, and made, with heart and mouth, in union with him, the acts agreed upon, of faith, of adoration, hope, and love, followed by the *Suscipe* of St. Ignatius, slowly repeated. Lastly, we all five together, kneeling by his bed, recited the prayers for those in their last agony.

The dear father did not, as far as we knew, any longer recognize or hear us. His breathing was comparatively good, and his pulse strong. He seemed likely to live still some hours, nevertheless, a quarter of an hour afterwards, in the peace of God, he breathed his last sigh.

Eternal rest grant unto him, O Lord.

And may perpetual light shine upon him.

May he rest in peace.

The death of Father Milleriot was announced by the following letter:

"The Fathers of the Company of Jesus, expelled from their residence in the rue de Sèvres, and dispersed, commend to your prayers the Rev. Father Louis Milleriot, who, half an hour after midnight, on the 2nd of March, at 26, rue de la Chaise, departed in the peace of the Lord. The funeral service will take place on Friday, the 4th of March, in the Church of St. Sulpice."

This invitation was responded to by multitudes of every rank, who, with pious eagerness, thronged around the poor coffin of the venerable dead, and followed it to the grave, feeling their hearts less filled with sadness than with a chastened joy. God had called to rest this good and faithful servant, glorified His Church in the life and death of this just man, and by the heartfelt homage rendered to the persecuted religious, the proscribed Jesuit, put to shame the hatred of triumphant impiety.

"The just man, dead, condemns the impious, living."*

He was gone, but his zeal for God had sown good seed, which was to spring up in due time. The conversion of the learned academician and lexicographer, M. Littré, with whom he had the most cordial relations, may in great measure be attributed to the friendship of a man for whom, long before he embraced his faith, he had the greatest veneration. On the day of Father Milleriot's death, the Father Superior having sent to inform M. Littré of the sorrowful event, sorrowful, above all, for the poor, received from him a letter, from which the following is an extract:

"To live long enough to see the death of men like Father Milleriot is to live too long. This is a heavy loss to me. His goodness to me was angelic. He loved me, although there was in me nothing to call forth this affection.

---

* "*Condemnat justus mortuus vivos impios.*"—1 Sap. iv. 16.

But although I did not deserve, I rejoiced in it as a free gift for which I was very grateful. *Grace is bestowed on us without our having merited it.* You know this, reverend father, better than I."

This letter has a special interest, as in some sense foreshadowing the great change which, by the grace of God, was to take place in his own convictions in the course of those remaining three months of his life, for he, too, when he wrote it, was nearing the threshold of eternity as well as the threshold of the Church.

To him the words might suitably have been applied, "At eventide there shall be light," while of the one who led him to it might be said with equal truth, "THE PATH OF THE JUST IS A SHINING LIGHT, WHICH SHINETH MORE AND MORE UNTO THE PERFECT DAY."

THE END.

Richardson and Son, Printers, Derby.

Richardson and Son's
NEW PUBLICATIONS.

THE PROBLEM SOLVED. Edited by LADY HERBERT. Crown 8vo, 450 pp., extra cloth, blocked black, with gold lettering, price 6s.

THE LIFE OF DOM BARTHOLOMEW OF THE MARTYRS, Religious of the Order of St. Dominic, Archbishop of Braga, in Portugal. Translated from his Biographies. By LADY HERBERT. In one thick volume, demy 8vo, price 12s. 6d.

HEAVEN OPENED: or our Home in Heaven, and the Way Thither. A Manual of Guidance for Devout Souls. By REV. FATHER COLLINS. Post 8vo, handsomely bound, price 5s.

LIGHTS AND SHADOWS OF HOME AFFECTIONS. A Moral Tale for the present epoch. Humbly Dedicated to her virtuous Queen, by the authoress of "Footsteps through Life," "Geraldine," &c. Crown 8vo, elegantly bound in cloth, price 7s.

BERNADETTE.—Sister Marie-Bernard. The Sequel to "Our Lady of Lourdes." By HENRI LASSERRE. Translated with the special permission of the author, by MRS. F. RAYMOND-BARKER. Foolscap 8vo, ornamental cloth, price 4s.

RICHARDSON AND SON'S PUBLICATIONS.

NEW SHILLING SERIES OF
CATHOLIC TALES.

Foolscap 8vo, handsomely bound in Cloth, with black printing on side, and lettered in gold.

The Queen's Confession; or, the Martyrdom of ST. JOHN NEPOMUCENE. By the Rev. J. J. K., O.S.F.

Elsie Mc'Dermott, the Little Watercress Girl. By M. A. Pennell.

Hilda's Victory; and Una's Repentance. Tales by M. F. S.

Little Musicians who became great Masters. First Series. Translated by Mrs. Townsend.

Little Musicians who became Great Masters. Second Series. Together with the FLOWERS of CHILDHOOD. Translated by Mrs. Townsend.

Ellerton Priory. A Tale. By the author of "Claire Maitland."

Little Flower Basket. By Canon Schmid.

The Search for Happiness, and other Tales for Young People.

Marie, the Fisherman's Daughter.

Godfrey, the Little Hermit. By Canon Schmid.

The Forest Pony, the Gipsy Boy, and other Tales by Lady Elizabeth Douglas.

The Gift: containing three interesting Tales.

Child-Life and its Lessons. Poetry, Original and Selected.

RICHARDSON AND SON'S PUBLICATIONS.

Just Published, Demy 18mo, handsomely bound in cloth,

PRICE 6d. EACH.

CATHOLIC TALES FOR THE YOUNG.

MORNING AND EVENING STAR.

CHRISTMAS DINNER.

HAWTHORN BUSH.

PEARL LOST & FOUND.

THE HOLY HOUSE.

MAURICE'S TRIAL.

CARRY'S TRIALS.

ALTAR FLOWERS.

A TALE OF THE CRUSADERS.

LIFE OF FREDDY WRAGG Br. M. Aloysius, Tertiary O.S.D., by Rev. H. Collins.

AUGUSTINE MC'NALLY, Tertiary, O.S.D., by the Rev. H. Collins.

WILLIE & HIS SISTERS.

☞ Will be followed by others uniform in size and binding.

MIDDLEFORD HALL. A Tale for Children. Edited by the Authoress of "ELLERTON PRIORY," "CLAIRE MAITLAND," &c. Handsomely bound in cloth, price 3s.

Graziella; or the History of a Broken Heart. An Episode of my Life. By A. De Lamartine. Translated from the French by J. B. S. Foolscap 8vo., cloth elegant, price 2s. 6d.

NUN OF THE ORDER OF THE VISITATION, Anne Madeleine de Remusat, of Marseilles, called the Second Margaret Mary of the Sacred Heart. *Foolscap 8vo, superfine cloth, price 3s. 6d.*

RICHARDSON AND SON'S PUBLICATIONS.

MINIATURE WORKS OF DEVOTIONAL AND PRACTICAL PIETY.

Handsomely bound in cloth, price 6d. each.

Heavenward. From "Heaven Opened." By REV. FATHER COLLINS.

Month of Jesus Christ. By S. Bonaventure.

Comfort for Mourners. By S. Francis of Sales. From his Letters. Translated by E. M. B.

Stations of the Passion as made in Jerusalem, and Select Devotions on the Passion, from the Prayers of S. Gertrude, O.S.B. Translated by Rev. H. Collins.

Holy Will of God: a Short Rule of Perfection. By the Rev. Father Benedict Canfield, Capuchin Friar. Translated by Father Collins.

The Our Father: Meditations on the Lord's Prayer. By St. Teresa. Translated by E. M. B.

The Quiet of the Soul. By Father John de Bovilla. To which is added, **Cure for Scruples.** By Dom Schram, O.S.B. Edited by the Rev. H. Collins.

Little Manual of Direction, for Priests, Religious Superiors, Novice-Masters and Mistresses, &c. By Dom Schram, O.S.B. Translated by Father Collins.

Visits to the Most Holy Sacrament, for every Day in the Month; also Preparation for and Thanksgiving after Communion. By S. Alphonsus Liguori. With an Appendix containing Benediction of the Blessed Sacrament. Cloth, price 6d.

Sacramentals of the Holy Catholic Church; being Instructions on the Prayers and Benedictions of the Church. By the Rev. W. J. Barry. *Royal 32mo, handsome cloth binding, red edges, 1s. 6d.*

www.ingramcontent.com/pod-product-compliance
Lightning Source LLC
Chambersburg PA
CBHW030337170426
43202CB00010B/1154